PET
Preliminary English Test

Practice
Tests ▶ Plus

Louise Hashemi
Barbara Thomas

Longman

Pearson Education Limited
Edinburgh Gate
Harlow
Essex CM20 2JE
England
And Associated Companies throughout the World.

www.longman.com

ISBN 0 582 34459 X

Set in 10.25pt Helvetica, 11pt Photina

Printed in Spain by Graficas Estella

First published 2000
Fifth impression 2003

Acknowledgements

We are grateful to the following for permission to reproduce copyright
photographs:

Ace Photo Agency for pages 14 right, 89 bottom; All Action for page 43
top; Bubbles Photo Library for pages 152 bottom, 154 top, 156 bottom;
James Davis Travel Photography for page 153 bottom; Eye Ubiquitous for
page 155 bottom; Sally & Richard Greenhill for page 152 top; Kit
Houghton for page 156 top; Penguin Longman Publishers for page 28;
PGL Travel Ltd for page 14 bottom left; Photofusion for page 14 top left;
The Photographers Library for page 154 bottom; Redferns for page 43
middle and bottom; Sporting Pictures (UK) Ltd for page 153 top; Still
Pictures for page 89 top; John Walmsley for page 155 top.

We are indebted to the University of Cambridge Local Examination
Syndicate (UCLES) for permission to reproduce PET/OMR answer sheets
for Reading Paper, Writing Paper and Listening Paper and UCLES EFL
material.

Illustrations by Gemini Design, Terry McKenna, Gary Rees, Liz Roberts
Designed by Michael Harris
Project managed by Linda Davey

Contents

Introduction

- This book contains five complete Practice Tests for PET which are the same as the exam.

- In Tests 1 and 2 there are exercises before each Part of the exam to help you understand what you have to do, and the best way to do it.

- In Tests 1 and 2 there are also extra language practice exercises to help you increase the language skills and knowledge you need to pass PET.

- In Test 3 there are exam tips to help you with each Part.

- Tests 4 and 5 offer you the opportunity to practise exactly what you will do in the exam.

- There is extra practice material for Writing Part 1.

- The English you need to pass PET is the same English you need for everyday situations, so using this book will help you both in the exam room and in the world outside.

Exam overview

Paper 1   Reading and Writing (1 hour 30 minutes)

Reading Parts 1–5

Part 1   5 signs with multiple-choice questions
Part 2   5 short texts with matching questions on 8 short texts
Part 3   1 longer factual text with 10 correct / incorrect questions
Part 4   1 longer text giving opinions or attitudes with 5 multiple-choice questions
Part 5   1 cloze text with 10 gaps and multiple-choice questions

Total = 25 marks

Writing Parts 1–3

Part 1   5 sentence transformations
Part 2   1 form-filling task with 10 spaces to fill
Part 3   1 letter to write, about 100 words long

Total = 25 marks

Paper 2   Listening (about 30 minutes)

Part 1   7 short conversations or pieces of speech with multiple-choice picture questions
Part 2   1 longer piece of speech with 6 multiple-choice questions
Part 3   1 longer piece of speech with 6 questions completing gaps in notes
Part 4   1 conversation with six correct / incorrect questions

Total = 25 marks

Paper 3   Speaking (10–12 minutes for two candidates together)

Part 1   Personal information, asking and answering questions (2–3 minutes)
Part 2   Discussing pictures (2–3 minutes)
Part 3   Talking about one of a pair of photographs (3 minutes)
Part 4   Discussion with the examiner related to Part 3 (3 minutes)

TEST 1

For each exam task in Test 1, there are exercises that:

- help you understand **what** you have to do in the exam

 Read the instructions to the exam task on the opposite page.

1 How many questions must you answer?
2 What does each question ask about?
3 Where do you mark your answers?

- show you **how** to approach each exam task – before you do the exam task, there is a summary and there are also tips to help you

 Key strategy
Underline the important points in the questions before you start, so you don't waste time reading through the wrong texts.

▶▶ Exam tip!

If you prefer, you can mark your answers on the paper and copy them onto the answer sheet when you have finished this Part.

- give you practice in the language you need to know for the exam.

The verbs *may*, *must* and *should* often appear in signs and questions about signs. Understanding the different meanings of these words will help you answer these questions.

The purpose of these exercises is to help you take the exam with confidence.

Grammar checklist

- modal verbs: *may*, *must(n't)*, *should(n't)*, *can't*
- *before* / *after* **-ing**
- *the* and *(a)n*
- *and* / *but* / *so* / *because*
- prepositions

- the passive
- expressions followed by **-ing**
- words that describe '*how much*'
- verbs followed by *to do*
- *if* (unreal situations)

Reading

Part 1

> In Part 1 you read signs, notices or labels which you might see in Britain.
> You choose the correct meaning for the signs from four explanations.

1 Read the instructions to the exam task on the opposite page.

1 How many questions must you answer?
2 What does each question ask about?
3 Where do you mark your answers?

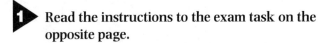

▶▶ Exam tip!

If you prefer, you can mark your answers on the paper and copy them onto the answer sheet when you have finished this Part.

2 Look at the example on the opposite page.

1 Where might you see this sign?
2 A is the correct answer. Let's decide why.
   Look at A.
   Underline the words which mean the same as DO NOT PARK.
   Underline the words which mean the same as BY THESE GATES.
3 Why is B wrong? Is the sign about a car park?
4 Why is C wrong? What does *park* mean in sentence C?
5 Why is D wrong? Does the sign say anything about closing the gates?

3 Look at Question 1.
   Find the right answer.

1 Where might you see this sign?
2 What words help you to decide? Underline them.
3 Where do you queue to buy tickets for next week?
4 Where do you pay to see tonight's performance?
5 Look at A, B, C and D. Which one means the same as the sign? Mark it. What words tell you? Underline them.
6 Look at the other sentences. Decide why they are wrong.

4 Language focus: *may*, *must* and *should*

> The verbs *may*, *must* and *should* often appear in signs and questions about signs. Understanding the different meanings of these words will help you answer these questions.

1 Can you find *may*, *must* or *should* in Question 2 of the exam task? Underline them.
2 *May*, *must* and *should* have different meanings.
   • You *may* leave your clothes in a locker =
     You *are allowed to* leave your clothes in a locker.
   • You *must* ask in the office =
     It is necessary that you ask in the office.
   • You *should* leave your clothes in a locker =
     It's a good idea to leave your clothes in a locker.

Now decide which is the right answer to Question 2, A, B, C or D.

5 Language practice

Rewrite these sentences in your notebook using *may*, *must* and *should*. Be careful not to change the meaning.

Example:
I advise you to catch the early train.
You should catch the early train.

1 You are allowed to picnic in this park.
2 We advise you to change your money at the bank.
3 It is essential to look after your luggage all the time.
4 It's a good idea to book a taxi in advance.
5 Visitors are permitted to use the canteen.
6 Students have to register in the office on arrival.

Part 1

Questions 1–5

- Look at the sign in each question.
- Someone asks you what it means.
- Mark the letter next to the correct explanation – **A**, **B**, **C** or **D** – **on your answer sheet.**

Example:

0

DO NOT PARK YOUR CAR BY THESE GATES

A Parking near these gates is forbidden.

B The entrance to the car park is through these gates.

C Do not bring your car into this park.

D Close these gates after parking your car.

Example answer:

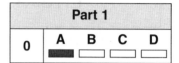

Part 1				
0	A	B	C	D

1

QUEUE HERE TO BOOK TICKETS IN ADVANCE.

FOR TONIGHT'S PERFORMANCE PAY AT BOX OFFICE.

A Tickets for all performances except tonight's are available here.

B Tickets paid for in advance may be collected from the box office.

C If you have already paid for your tickets, collect them here.

D If you have booked tickets, pay for them here.

2

SWIMMING POOL

THE OFFICE KEEPS CLOTHES LEFT IN LOCKERS FOR TWO WEEKS ONLY

A You may leave your clothes in a locker for two weeks.

B You will not find your lost clothes in the office after two weeks.

C You must ask in the office before leaving clothes in a locker.

D You should leave your clothes in a locker if the office is closed.

6 ▶ Finish the task.

Look at the other signs (3–5) below. Choose the correct answer for each one and mark them on your answer sheet.

3

EXIT

THIS DOOR MAY
ONLY BE USED
BY STAFF
AFTER SIX P.M.

A You must ask a member of staff to unlock the door.

B People who work here must leave the building by six p.m.

C This is the only door which staff may use in the evening.

D You may use this door in the evening if you work here.

4

WILLIAM'S BAKERS

**HAS MOVED.
OUR NEW SHOP IS
OPPOSITE LIBRARY.**

A The library is no longer near the baker's shop.

B William's Bakers now has two shops.

C William's Bakers is across the road from the library.

D The library is next door to the baker's shop.

5

**DO NOT USE
EQUIPMENT IN THIS
BOX BEFORE
READING
INSTRUCTIONS**

A Do not remove the equipment from the box before reading the instructions.

B Read the instructions before using the equipment.

C Do not put the equipment in the box without the instructions.

D Put the equipment in the box after using it.

1 ▶ Vocabulary: words you see in signs

The words in the box often appear on the signs and notices in Part 1. Choose the correct word for each gap in the notices below. The first one is done for you.

assistant	available	arrival	cancelled
credit card	discount	emergency	~~entrance~~
forbidden	~~luggage~~	responsible	permitted
on time	out of order	reception	urgent

1 This .entrance. is for passengers without ..luggage... only.
2 This lift is .... Please ask an .... for help if you cannot use the stairs.
3 For very .... enquiries, please ring the bell on the .... desk.
4 10% .... on group bookings. Pay by ....
5 All the trains are running .... today except the 10.05 which is ....
6 At weekends the doctor is only .... in an ....
7 On ...., visiting students must wait here to be met by the teacher who is .... for sports.
8 Smoking is .... during lectures but is .... during the coffee break.

Where might you see these signs (1–8 above)?

2 ▶ Grammar: *before / after + -ing*

Signs often tell you how to do something. They may use the words *before* or *after + -ing*.

a) Look at Question 5 in the exam task on the opposite page. How many examples can you find of *before* or *after + -ing*?

b) Make sentences in your notebook using *before* or *after + -ing*.

   Example:
   read the instructions / use the equipment (before)
   Read the instructions before using the equipment.

1 take a shower / use the swimming pool (before)
2 clear the table / eat a meal (after)
3 ask permission / use the telephone (before)
4 pick up your rubbish / have a picnic (after)
5 wash your hands / prepare a meal (before)
6 lock the door / use the sports hall (after)
7 buy a ticket / get on the train (before)

3 ▶ Grammar: *the* and *a(n)*

The words *the* and *a(n)* are often left out in signs and notices.

a) Look at the signs in the exam task on pages 7 and 8 and find places where *the* and *a(n)* are left out. Write them in.

b) Read these signs and add *the* or *a(n)* where necessary to make sentences.

1
> **OFFICE IS CLOSED**
>
> **GO TO MAIN RECEPTION DESK AT FRONT OF BUILDING**

2
> IN EMERGENCY
> USE TELEPHONE IN
> HALL TO CALL
> HOSTEL MANAGER

3
> **PLEASE USE OTHER WAITING ROOM IF YOU HAVE APPOINTMENT WITH DENTIST**

4
> **Passengers with return ticket must show it to driver**

5
> IF RECEIPT IS NEEDED
> ASK ASSISTANT
> WHEN PAYING

Part 2

> In Part 2, each question describes different people.
> You match the people to the texts on the opposite page.

1 Read the instructions to the exam task on the opposite page.

1 How many questions are there?

2 What do all the people want?

3 What are the texts about?

4 How many texts are there?

5 What do you have to decide?

6 Where do you mark your answers?

2 Look at Questions 6–10 on the opposite page and think about the information given.

Each question describes a different person or group of people. Look at the pictures first. Think about the kind of people they show. All the people are looking for something different. For example, in Question 6 we can underline the things which are important for Charlotte and David.

6 Charlotte and David want to spend the weekend in the <u>city centre</u> with their six-month-old <u>baby</u>. They want to be <u>near the railway station</u> and be able to <u>walk everywhere</u>. They will eat in restaurants.

Now underline the important parts of Questions 7–10.

3 Language focus: hotel facilities

> In Part 2, the texts are often about facilities for tourists. The texts you are going to read are all about hotels.

Match the words and phrases in the box with the hotel signs below.

restaurant   gym   swimming pool   telephone in room   car park city centre – 3kms   bicycles for hire   lift   television in room   entertainment garden   golf   railway station – 5 mins   tennis courts

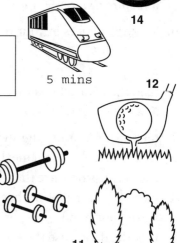

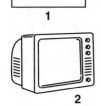

Part 2

Questions 6–10

- The people below all want to find somewhere to stay.
- On the next page there are descriptions of eight places to stay.
- Decide which place (**letters A–H**) would be the most suitable for each of the following people (**numbers 6–10**).
- For each of these numbers mark the correct letter on your answer sheet.

Example answer:

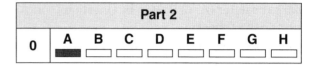

Part 2								
0	A	B	C	D	E	F	G	H

6  Charlotte and David want to spend the weekend in the city centre with their six-month-old baby. They want to be near the railway station and be able to walk everywhere. They will eat in restaurants.

7  Michael wants to spend the weekend somewhere quiet in the country which has a car park. He would like to swim but is not interested in other sports.

8  Mary hasn't been well and wants a quiet break in the countryside. She would like to stay somewhere where there are organised activities so that she can meet other people.

9  Sandra and Martin don't want to be further than ten kilometres from the city. They are coming by car and want to park in the hotel and have dinner there. They like to swim every day.

10  Pam and Daniel have three children who enjoy sport. They want to stay somewhere in the city which provides lunch and dinner and has a car park.

4 ▶ **Look at the texts below.**

1   Look at Question 6 again. Charlotte and David want to be in the city centre. Mark which hotels are in the city.

2   Which texts do you need to read carefully?

3   Which of the hotels is best for Charlotte and David? (Remember they want to walk around the city centre!)

4   Check your answer. Is the hotel near the railway station? Do Charlotte and David want to eat at the hotel? Is the hotel suitable for the baby?

5   Mark the letter (A, B, C, etc.) by Question 6 on your answer sheet.

6   Now look at Question 7. Michael wants to be in the country. Mark which hotels are in the country. Read these texts carefully.

7   Which is the best hotel for Michael?

8   Check your answer. Does it have a car park? Does it have a swimming pool?

9   Mark the letter (A, B, C, etc.) by Question 7 on your answer sheet.

▶▶ **Exam tip!**

You must have a different answer for each question. If you think the same hotel is the answer to two questions, you must check again, because one of them is wrong!

5 ▶ **Finish the exam task.**
Look at the important points you underlined for Questions 8–10. Use them to help you decide which hotels are the most suitable for the other people. Then mark your answers on your answer sheet.

▶ **Key strategy**
Underline the important points in the questions before you start, so you don't waste time reading through the wrong texts.

A   **The Regent Hotel** is about a ten-minute drive from the city centre and has its own gym, tennis courts and entertainment at weekends. Guests can eat all their meals here – breakfast, lunch and dinner. There is a large car park. All rooms have their own television and telephone.

B   **Somerset Lodge** is between two farms. The hotel arranges competitions, dances, film shows and other events which you can attend if you wish or you can walk in the large gardens and enjoy the scenery. It is especially popular with people travelling alone and has a lift. All meals are available on request.

C   **Castle Hotel** is popular with visitors travelling by car as it is close to all the main roads and has a large car park. It is outside the city but hotel staff can collect you from the station if you don't drive and arrange trips in the area by coach. Breakfast only is served but there are two good restaurants nearby.

D   **Marwood House** is about three kilometres from the city centre and has a large car park. It is easy to drive to the city's main car park or into the surrounding countryside. There is a swimming pool in the next street. Dinner is available if booked in advance.

E   **George Hotel** is on the south side of the city – just a short taxi ride from the railway station and places of interest. It has events such as talks and shows every evening which are popular both with guests and local people. Parking is available in nearby streets. Breakfast only is provided.

F   **Haywood House** was once a family home. It is in the middle of the hills twenty kilometres from the city so it is a peaceful place to spend a few days. It has a restaurant serving breakfast, lunch and dinner, plenty of car parking spaces and very good sports facilities including golf, tennis and a swimming pool.

G   **Dunstan Lodge** is a family hotel in the city centre near the market square where a range of restaurants are available. It is five minutes' walk from the railway and bus station and close to all the city's facilities. Bicycles are available for hire. No car parking or meals except breakfast.

H   **The Four Seasons Hotel** is in the countryside about five kilometres from the city centre. It is very near the motorway with plenty of parking space so it is convenient for drivers. Meals are not available but there is a fast-food restaurant just two kilometres along the motorway where breakfast, lunch and dinner are available.

Extra language practice

 Speaking about hotel facilities

Look at the signs for hotel facilities on page 10. You are going to stay in a hotel. Decide which five of the facilities are most important for you and put a tick (✓) next to them.

Now work with a partner. Tell each other which hotel facilities are most important for you and why. Use the language in the box to help you.

Useful language
I want ...   I need (to) ...   I like ...   I'd like (to) ...   I'm interested in ...   I enjoy ...

Example: 'A swimming pool is important for me because I love swimming.'

 Grammar: *and / but / so / because*

These words are important to make sense of a sentence. Look at these sentences from the questions and texts. Match the two halves. The first one is done for you.

1 They want to be near the railway station and   a) there are two good restaurants nearby.
2 Breakfast only is served but   b) it is close to all the main roads.
3 It is very near the motorway so   c) be able to walk everywhere.
4 Castle Hotel is popular with visitors travelling   d) it is convenient for drivers.
   by car because

Now do the same with these.

5 This hotel is near the airport so   e) the owners go on holiday.
6 The restaurant is very small but   f) it is very popular with business travellers.
7 The hotel is closed in January because   g) have lovely views of the sea.
8 The rooms are very comfortable and   h) serves excellent meals.

Complete the following sentences in your notebook using your own ideas.

9 I complained about my room because ....
10 The hotel was full so ....
11 I prefer to stay in the city centre and ....
12 The manager didn't speak much English but ....

Vocabulary: prepositions

Choose a word from the box to fill each space in the sentences below. They are all used in the same way somewhere in the texts about hotels. The first one is done for you.

between   from   from   in   in   ~~near~~   of   of   on   with

1 My office is ..*near*.. the shops.
2 I can't collect you .... the airport because I have guests.
3 My school is .... the north side .... the town.
4 My house is about fifteen minutes drive .... the bus station.
5 There are many places .... interest .... this area.
6 The new government building is .... two parks.
7 My uncle bought a new house .... the countryside when he retired.
8 Baseball is becoming more popular .... young people in Europe.

Part 3

In Part 3 there are some statements about a text.
You read the text and decide whether the statements are true or false.

 1 Read the instructions to the exam task on the opposite page.

1 How many statements are there?
2 What are the statements about?
3 What do you have to read?
4 What do you have to decide?
5 When do you mark *A* on your answer sheet?
6 When do you mark *B* on your answer sheet?

 2 Read statements 11–20 to get a good idea what the text is about.
Find which statement is about each of the following topics and write the number next to it. The first one is done for you.

a) places to stay   *17*
b) how the day is organised
c) cancellations
d) what happens if it rains
e) what you need to take
f) when to pay
g) when they are open
h) staff qualifications
i) method of payment
j) who the courses are suitable for

 3 Now read the text on the opposite page.
For each of the statements 11–20, mark on the text where you think the answer is. The first two are done for you.

▶▶ Exam tip!

You don't need to understand every word in the text to answer the questions. Some parts of the text aren't tested so don't worry about them.

 4 **Language focus: making adjectives negative**

Look at statement 13. *Unsuitable* means the same as *not suitable*. So, Courses **aren't suitable** for = Courses are *unsuitable for*.

a) Read the statements again. Can you find any other negative adjectives?

b) Rewrite the following sentences in your notebook using the negative form of the underlined adjective. You will need to use: *im-*, *in-* and *un-*.

Example:
It isn't underlined necessary to bring equipment.
It's unnecessary to bring equipment.

1 My answers weren't correct.
....
2 Some of the staff aren't qualified.
....
3 It isn't possible for us to arrange other accommodation.
....
4 Luxury accommodation isn't available near our camps.
....

 5 Finish the exam task.
Look at each statement again, find the right part of the text and decide whether the statement is correct or incorrect. Mark your answer on your answer sheet.

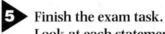 **Key strategy**

Read the statements before you read the text. Mark the parts of the text which contain the information you need.

Part 3

Questions 11–20

- Look at the statements about a company which organises sports camps.
- Read the text below to decide if each statement is correct or incorrect.
- If it is correct, mark **A on your answer sheet.**
- If it is incorrect, mark **B on your answer sheet.**

Example answer:

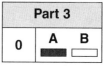

11   Some centres are open all winter.

12   The activities available depend on the weather.

13   Action Sports Camps courses are unsuitable for people who are excellent at sport.

14   You need to have your own sports equipment.

15   Children and adults spend some time together each day.

16   Some of the staff are unqualified.

17   Action Sports Camps only recommend accommodation of a high quality.

18   You have to pay the total fee one month after you book.

19   Action Sports Camps charge you more if you pay with your credit card.

20   If you cancel three weeks before your camp, you will get half your money back.

ACTION SPORTS CAMPS

Action Sports Camps provide activity holidays for children aged over five and adults. We offer training in over twenty sports at ten different centres throughout the UK. All the centres are open from April until October and <u>some open during the winter for weekend courses</u>. The sports offered differ from one centre to another so if you want to do something in particular you should check our colour brochure.

The camps are not just limited to outdoor sports – we cover a wide range of indoor activities as well. So <u>if the rain comes</u>, the camps continue although you may have to take off your football boots and pick up a squash racket instead. With the experience we've gained over the years, we put together the right mix of sport and activities providing sport for all, not just for those who are brilliant at athletics. It is unnecessary to bring any equipment because it is all provided.

We work in small groups, children working with others of their own age, but we do all come together for social activities and meals. So, different members of a family can make their own individual choices but they get a chance to exchange their experiences later on.

Our centres offer first-class accommodation, food and facilities – and the staff are first-class too. Qualified teachers or professionals receive training from us and many work with us year after year. We always employ qualified staff for activities such as swimming, trampolining and gymnastics but some of the assistants organising the children's games are students, many of whom came to the camp themselves when they were younger.

At most of our centres, accommodation is in a hostel or tents. It is not possible for us to arrange other accommodation but we can send you a list of what is available in the area. Most of the places are recommended to us, but not all, so we are not responsible for the quality of the accommodation on this list. Luxury accommodation is not available near our camps.

To book a place at a sports camp, complete the form and send it with a cheque for the deposit to the address below. The rest of the fee can be paid at any time but we must receive it at least one month before your camp. Please note, to keep costs down, you are charged 2.5% extra by us if you pay with your credit card. You will receive a letter of confirmation within ten days of sending your form. Cancellations made up to a month before the camp are refunded in full apart from a 5% administration fee. Fifty per cent of the fee is refunded if a cancellation is made up to two weeks before the date of the camp. After that no refunds can be given.

▷▷ Extra language practice

1 ▶ Speaking about likes and dislikes

a) Look at the table below. Tick the boxes to show which of these adjectives you could use to describe staff, accommodation, activities and weather. The first one is done for you.

	staff	accommodation	activities	weather
boring	✓		✓	
cold				
comfortable				
warm				
helpful				
interesting				
rainy				
sunny				
friendly				

Which of the adjectives above can you make negative by using *un-?*

b) Now work with a partner. You both recently went to a different Action Sports Camp. Compare your experiences.

Student A: You enjoyed yourself very much. Talk about why you liked it. Use the language in the table above to help you.

Example:
'*I had a great time. The activities were really interesting.*'

Student B: You didn't have a good time. Talk about why you didn't enjoy yourself. Use the language in the table above to help you.

Example:
'*My camp was awful. The activities were boring.*'

2 ▶ Grammar: forming the passive

Look at Question 19 on page 15:
Action Sports Camps charge you more if you pay with your credit card.
This is correct because it means the same as
You are charged 2.5% extra by us if you pay with your credit card.

Now rewrite the following sentences in your notebook using the words given. Put the verb into the passive and decide if you need to use *by*.

Example:
My brother recommended this pop festival to me.
This pop festival *was recommended to me by my brother.*

1 The organisers invite bands from all over the world.
  Bands from all over the world ....
2 Our local music shop sells tickets.
  Tickets ....
3 But my friend gave me a ticket.
  But I ....
4 He also offered me a lift in his car.
  I ....
5 A man told us where to put our tent.
  We ....
6 The campsite owner provided water for cooking.
  Water for cooking ....
7 It rained, but the bad weather didn't spoil our weekend.
  It rained, but our weekend ....
8 The organisers asked us to take all our rubbish away with us.
  We ....

3 ▶ Vocabulary: words that mean the same

In Part 3 the statements often contain words and phrases which are different from those in the text but which have the same meaning.

Choose a word or phrase from the box to replace one word in each sentence 1–8 without changing the meaning.

advises	book	closed	employees	fill in
less expensive	not allowed	~~pleasant~~	take back

Example: *pleasant*
There are some (nice) shops in the city centre.

1 This office is shut for lunch.
2 All the staff had a pay rise last month.
3 Don't forget to return your library book when you're in town.
4 I'd like to reserve three seats for Monday's performance, please.
5 It is cheaper to go to London by bus than by train.
6 Students are forbidden to take mobile phones into the exam room.
7 Please complete this form before the plane lands.
8 The college recommends that students should apply early for popular courses.

Part 4

> In Part 4 you read a text.
> You then answer some questions about it by choosing A, B, C, or D.

1 Read the instructions to the exam task below.

1 What do you have to read?
2 What do you have to do?
3 Where do you mark your answers?

2 Read the text quickly and think about these questions.

1 What sort of work does the writer do?
2 Why is he writing this text?
3 Who might want to read it?

3 Language focus: feelings

Part 4 often uses words which show how people feel about things.

Look at these phrases from the text. Some of them are about feeling happy and some of them are about feeling bad. Mark (+) by the happy ones and (–) by the bad ones. This will help you to understand the text. The first one is done for you.

1 *a wonderful way to earn one's living*   +
2 *lots of great things*
3 *What I really like is*
4 *when I'm bored*
5 *doing something I enjoy*
6 *Unfortunately*
7 *it's too late*
8 *I feel increasingly stressed*

Part 4

Questions 21–25

- Read the text and questions below.
- For each question, mark the letter next to the correct answer – **A**, **B**, **C** or **D** – **on your answer sheet.**

Example answer:

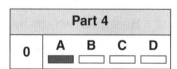

Part 4			
0	A	B	C	D

People think being an artist must be a wonderful way to earn one's living. And of course, there are lots of great things about working for oneself, at home, alone. What I really like is that nobody tells me what time to start in the morning, or what to wear, or whether I can take the afternoon off and go to a football match.

But then, I have no one to chat with when I'm bored, no one to discuss last night's match with during the lunch-hour. Sure, I can spend the afternoon doing something I enjoy like swimming, or walking the dog, or even sleeping, if I choose. But the work will still be there when I do finally get back home. And it's still got to be finished in time.

Unfortunately, working at home means that people can always find me, whether I'm bored or not and once I've answered the doorbell, it's too late - my thoughts have been interrupted. No one would dream of calling in if I worked in an office, but I find myself making cups of coffee and listening to friends' troubles. As they talk my ideas disappear and I feel increasingly stressed thinking of my work waiting to be done.

Look at Questions 21–25.

It is important to understand the questions before reading the text in more detail. This exercise will help you to think about the questions.

Underline the best word or phrase to complete each sentence.

1 Look at Question 21. This is always a general question.

This question asks about the writer's *life / purpose / job*.

2 Look at Question 22. This is usually a general question.

This question asks about *who wrote the text / when the text was written / what the text tells you*.

3 Look at Question 23. This question always asks about detail or opinion.

This question asks about the writer's *feelings / home / friends*.

4 Look at Question 24. This question always asks about detail or opinion.

This question asks about the writer's *pictures / conversations / thoughts*.

5 Look at Question 25. This is always a general question.

This question asks about what the writer *will do / might do / has done*.

▶▶ **Exam tip!**

Questions 21 and 25 are always about the whole text. Don't try to answer them by looking at the first and last sentences only!

5 Finish the exam task.

Read the text again carefully and choose the correct answer for each question. Mark your answers on your answer sheet.

▶ **Key strategy**
Read the text quickly to get a general idea. Read the questions carefully, then go back to the text and look for the answers.

---

21 What is the writer trying to do in the text?

A encourage readers to work at home

B explain why he has changed his job

C describe his working life

D say how he would like to work

22 What can the reader learn from the text?

A how to start working for oneself

B what it's like to work at home

C why the writer decided to work for himself

D how artists become successful

23 What does the writer like about his life?

A He has plenty of opportunities for sport.

B He is his own boss.

C He can see people when he wants to.

D He has a comfortable place to work.

24 What does the writer imagine he might do with colleagues?

A have meals in restaurants

B go to the swimming pool

C spend time in the countryside

D talk about sport

25   Which of these notices would be most useful for the writer to put on his door?

A

> I'm working –
> please don't
> disturb

B

> *Please call at my*
> *office for an*
> *appointment*

C

> **Please knock**
> **before entering**

D

> **NO VISITORS**
> **ALLOWED DURING**
> **OFFICE HOURS**

▷▷ **Extra language practice**

 Grammar: expressions followed by *-ing*

The text on page 17 is by a man writing about his feelings. Here are some ways you can say what you feel. They are all followed by the *-ing* form of the verb. Complete the sentences in your notebook with true information about yourself.

1   I really like ....
2   I don't enjoy ....
3   I often spend the evening ....
4   I'm looking forward to ....
5   I hate ....
6   I'm bored of ....
7   I sometimes worry about ....
8   I'm quite keen on ....
9   I really dislike ....
10   I feel very happy about ....

 Vocabulary: jobs

In the exam you often have to read, write or speak about jobs.

Match the words in the box with the job titles below.

| to mark   to shoot   to serve   to deliver   to land |
| to interview   book   aeroplane   goal   customer |
| parcel   camera   postcode   receipt   match |
| classroom   news   departure |

1   postman/woman   4   TV presenter
2   shop assistant   5   footballer
3   teacher   6   pilot

 Speaking about jobs

Work with a partner. You should each choose a job from the list in Exercise 2 but don't tell your partner which one. Imagine what you do every day.

• What time do you get up?
• How many hours do you spend at work?
• What is the best / worst thing about your job?

Describe your job to your partner and see if he / she can guess your job. Use the language in the box to help you.

Useful language

I get up at ...
I usually ...
I like ...
I often spend my day ...
I don't enjoy ...
The best / worst thing about my job is ...

Example:
'I get up very early. I have to walk a long way.'

Part 5

1 ▶ Read the instructions to the exam task on the opposite page.

1 What do you have to read?
2 What do you have to choose?
3 Where do you mark your answers?

2 ▶ Look at the text heading and make guesses about the text.
Can you guess what you will learn about the student? Tick the things you think you will find out.

1 Why did she choose her course?
2 Where is she going for her holidays?
3 What does she do in her spare time?
4 What subjects does the course include?
5 What are her parents' jobs?
6 How do the students study?
7 How useful will the course be?

3 ▶ Read the text quickly and check your guesses.
Which of your guesses were correct? Don't worry about the numbered spaces for now.

4 ▶ Look at the example (0).
Read the first sentence of the text carefully. What is the answer to Question (0)?

5 ▶ Look at Questions 26–35.
For each question, read the whole of the sentence which contains the space. Choose your answers for the ones you are certain about. Write the words in the spaces – they may help you to understand the text.

▶▶ **Exam tip!**

Always look at the words after each space as well as the words before it.

6 ▶ Finish the exam task.
Now go back and guess the other answers. When you have done all the questions, mark your answers on your answer sheet. Check that you are putting them in the right place.

> **Key strategy**
> Read the whole text before you start thinking about the spaces. Then choose the best answer for each space. Leave the ones you are not sure about until the end – the answers may become clearer then.

Part 5

Questions 26–35

- Read the text below and choose the correct word for each space.
- For each question, mark the letter next to the correct word – **A**, **B**, **C** or **D** – on **your answer sheet**.

Example answer:

Part 5				
0	A	B	C	D
	▬	☐	☐	☐

Life at university – a student writes

I enjoyed business studies at school and wanted to **(0)** .... my knowledge of the subject so I decided to study it at university. Also I knew it would be **(26)** .... later when I looked for a job. At first, the course wasn't quite **(27)** .... I had expected because it didn't cover the subjects I was particularly interested **(28)** .... We spent lots of time studying a range of subjects **(29)** .... law and economics but I soon **(30)** .... these are things you need to understand.

In class we work in groups, preparing ideas, we then **(31)** .... them with the others. Now we're learning how to make business plans and we can see how they would **(32)** .... apply to the world of business. We have a very busy **(33)** .... life at university so whatever subject you study, you must be **(34)** .... on it or you won't make yourself find the **(35)** .... to study.

0	**A** increase	**B** grow	**C** fill	**D** correct
26	**A** likely	**B** useful	**C** possible	**D** hopeful
27	**A** that	**B** which	**C** what	**D** than
28	**A** by	**B** with	**C** of	**D** in
29	**A** so	**B** as	**C** such	**D** like
30	**A** explained	**B** realised	**C** showed	**D** believed
31	**A** divide	**B** join	**C** share	**D** add
32	**A** actually	**B** just	**C** presently	**D** exactly
33	**A** party	**B** evening	**C** social	**D** free
34	**A** glad	**B** keen	**C** clever	**D** quick
35	**A** time	**B** period	**C** day	**D** hour

Extra language practice

 Speaking about studying

Think about the following questions.

• What subject would you like to study at university? Why?
• How many years will you have to study?
• Do you think it will be easy or difficult?
• If you are already at university, tell each other about your course and what you want to do when you finish.

When you are ready, discuss the questions with your partner.

> **Useful language**
>
> I'm very interested in ...
> My favourite subject is ...
> I want to do a course in ...
> I hope to become a ...
> I aim to qualify as a ...

 Vocabulary: similar meanings

> **Part 5 tests words with similar meanings.**

For each group of four words below, check that you know the differences in their meanings and how they are used in sentences. Underline the word which best fits each space. Use a dictionary to help you. The first one is done for you.

1 <u>spend</u>   buy   charge   pay
How much did you .... on that new tennis racket?

2 remember   revise   report   remind
Please .... me to phone the airport tomorrow morning.

3 told   talked   said   spoke
The doctor .... my father to take more exercise.

4 journey   voyage   tour   trip
My sister is going on a .... of Scotland this summer.

5 view   sight   scene   scenery
There is a lot of wonderful .... in Switzerland.

6 fearful   nervous   afraid   frightening
This story is too .... for small children.

7 opinion   thought   idea   feeling
There are too many cars on the roads, in my ....

8 problem   mistake   fault   cause
We're late because the train was cancelled, it's not our ....

9 study   training   learning   practice
You have to do a .... course before you can work as a teacher.

10 divide   join   add   share
There weren't enough books for everyone so they had to .... with each other.

 Grammar: words that describe 'how much'

> **The words below are often tested in the exam. Check that you know how they are used.**

> enough   more   much   so   such   than
> too   ~~very~~

Complete the sentences with a word from the box.

1 The test was ..<u>very</u>.. difficult but I passed it.
2 She doesn't like Chinese food as .... as I do.
3 I rarely see new films. I wish I could go to the cinema .... often.
4 My cousin is .... tall that she has a problem finding clothes to fit.
5 This suitcase is .... small for all the clothes I want to take.
6 She is .... a bossy person that nobody wants to be friends with her.
7 The swimming pool isn't big .... for international competitions.
8 My new music teacher is friendlier .... my last one.

Writing

Part 1

> In Part 1 you read some sentences and then you rewrite them using a different grammar pattern.

 Read the instructions to the exam task below.

1 How many sentences are there?
2 What are the sentences about?
3 What do you have to do?
4 Where do you write your answers?
5 How much do you write there?
6 Where can you do your rough work?

 Look at the example.

1 Read the first sentence. What information does it give you about the guesthouse?
2 Now read the second sentence. Does it give you the same information as the first sentence?

3 ▶ **Look at Question 1.**

1 Read the first sentence. What information does it give you about the guesthouse?
2 Now read the beginning of the second sentence. How does it begin?
3 How can you complete it? Write your answer.
4 Check your answer. Does your sentence give the same information as the first sentence? Is the grammar correct?

▶▶ **Exam tip!**

In this part of the exam you will lose marks if your grammar is not correct. If you are not sure about your answer, write it on the exam paper first and read it carefully before you copy it onto your answer sheet.

Part 1

Questions 1–5

- Here are some sentences about a guesthouse.
- For each question, finish the second sentence so that it means the same as the first.
- The second sentence is started for you. **Write only the missing words on your answer sheet.**
- You may use this page for any rough work.

> **Example:** There is a games room in this guesthouse.
>
> **This guesthouse** ..*has a games room*...

1 The guesthouse is called 'Sunshine Cottage'.

The name ....

4 ▶ Language focus 1: grammar patterns

In Part 1, the same grammar patterns are often tested. It is a good idea to study these patterns so that you can recognise them.

a) Look at the example on page 23 again.

The pattern here is: *There is an X in Y. = Y has an X.*

What is the pattern in Question 1? Write it here:
X is called Y. = The name ....

b) Read the ten sentences below. There are five pairs which have the same meanings. Can you find them?

Example: 1, 7

1 Her name is Jane.
2 I was told the news by Jane.
3 It was essential to talk to Jane about the news.
4 I haven't met Jane before.
5 I had to talk to Jane about the news.

6 Jane is popular with everybody.
7 She is called Jane.
8 Jane told me about the news.
9 This is the first time I have met Jane.
10 Everybody likes Jane.

5 ▶ Finish the exam task.

Write the answers to Questions 2–5 on your answer sheet. Remember you can write your answers on the exam paper first if you wish and then copy them.

▶ Key strategy
Think carefully about the meaning of the first sentence. When you complete the second sentence, make sure it means the same as the first one.

2 I haven't stayed here before.

This is ....

3 I was told about it by a friend.

A friend ....

4 The town is popular with foreign tourists.

Foreign tourists ....

5 It is essential to book your room in advance.

You ....

6 Language focus 2: correcting mistakes

Read these pairs of sentences. They should mean the same. The second sentence in each pair is wrong. Can you correct it?

Example:
He is called Robert.
His name is ~~called~~ Robert.

1 This car is too small for my family.
This car is not enough big for my family.

2 That factory is owned by my uncle.
My uncle owned that factory.

3 The town has several pleasant parks.
There are several pleasant parks.

4 The tourist asked 'Where is the railway station?'
The tourist asked where was the railway station.

5 It isn't necessary to book a ticket for this show.
You mustn't book a ticket for this show.

7 Check your answers to the exam task.
Read your answers and correct any mistakes. Exchange your answers with another student and correct any mistakes you find.

 Extra language practice

Grammar: modal verbs

Part 1 often tests modal verbs. Some of the important ones are in the box below.

can't ~~must~~ mustn't need shouldn't needn't should

a) Look at your answers to the exam task on the opposite page. Which of them contained a modal verb?

b) Complete the second sentence so that it means the same as the first. Use one of the verbs in the box above. The first one is done for you.

1 It is essential to check in your luggage an hour before your flight.
You .*must.* check in your luggage an hour before your flight.

2 Smoking is forbidden in the youth hostel.
You .... smoke in the youth hostel.

3 It isn't necessary to take your own towel to that swimming pool.
You .... take your own towel to that swimming pool.

4 Customers are advised to check their change before leaving the shop.
You .... check your change before leaving the shop.

5 It is impossible to get a ticket for the Cup Final.
You .... get a ticket for the Cup Final.

6 It is necessary for all children to learn to use a computer.
All children .... to learn to use a computer.

7 Students are advised not to leave all their revision until the day before the exam.
Students .... leave all their revision until the day before the exam.

c) Work with a partner. Look at the notice below. Take turns to tell each other what the notice says using the modal verbs.

Example:
'You should check the weather forecast before leaving.'

♦ WALKERS ARE ADVISED TO CHECK THE WEATHER FORECAST BEFORE LEAVING.
♦ IT IS ESSENTIAL TO TAKE WARM CLOTHES.
♦ WALKERS ARE ADVISED NOT TO WALK ALONE.
♦ IT ISN'T NECESSARY TO WALK WITH AN ORGANISED GROUP.
♦ WALKERS ARE FORBIDDEN TO LEAVE THE PATH.
♦ WALKERS ARE ADVISED TO TAKE A MAP.
♦ IT IS IMPOSSIBLE TO USE A MOBILE PHONE ON THE MOUNTAIN.
♦ IT IS NECESSARY TO WEAR GOOD BOOTS.

Part 2

> In Part 2 you are given a form.
> You have to fill in information about yourself on the form.

 1 Read the instructions to the exam task on the opposite page.

1 Where are you?
2 What kind of form is it?
3 What do you have to do?
4 Where do you write your answers?
5 Where can you do your rough work?

 2 Language focus: nationalities

In Part 2 you often need to write the names of different countries and languages. It's important to spell them correctly and to remember to use capital letters at the beginning.

Complete the table. The first line has been done for you.

country	nationality	language
Argentina	Argentinian	Spanish
Brazil		
	Chilean	
Egypt		
		French
		Greek
Italy		
	Japanese	
Poland		
		Russian
	Spanish	
	Turkish	

 3 Look at the completed form below. Say what is wrong with the answers to each question.

Example:
(6) She hasn't written her surname.

NEWTON LANGUAGE CENTRE

MAIN STREET
NEWTON   NT4 5TG   ENGLAND
UK

Library users' questionnaire

Full name: **(6)** *Maria* ....

Home address (including country): **(7)** *10 avenue Berlioz, 20313 Villeneuve* ....

....

Date of birth (day/month/year): **(8)** *16th July* ....

Sex: **(9)** *girl* ....

Nationality: **(10)** *France* ....

Which language(s) do you speak (apart from English)? **(11)** *french and spanish* ....

....

How many years have you studied English? **(12)** *eigt* ....

What is your job in your country (or what job do you hope to do after leaving school)?
(13) *hotel* ....

What kind of fiction do you like reading?
(14) *books about cooking and music* ....

Signature **(15)** *M.J.* ....

---

4 ▶ Write your answers.

Now fill in your own answers for Questions 6–15. For Questions 6–10 you must give true answers. For Questions 11–15 you can use your imagination if you want. Write your answers on your answer sheet. Remember, you can write them on the exam paper first if you wish and then copy them.

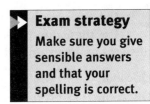

Part 2

Questions 6–15

- You are studying English in a language school in England.
- The school library gives you a questionnaire to complete.
- Look at the questionnaire and answer each question.
- **Write your answers on your answer sheet.**
- You may use this page for any rough work.

NEWTON LANGUAGE CENTRE

MAIN STREET
NEWTON   NT4 5TG   ENGLAND
UK

Library users' questionnaire

Full name: (**6**) ....

Home address (including country): (**7**) ....

....

Date of birth (day/month/year): (**8**) ....

Sex: (**9**) ....

Nationality: (**10**) ....

Which language(s) do you speak (apart from English)? (**11**) ....

....

How many years have you studied English? (**12**) ....

What is your job in your country (or what job do you hope to do after leaving school)?

(**13**) ....

What kind of fiction do you like reading?

(**14**) ....

Signature (**15**) ....

5 Check your answers.

Use these questions to help you check your answers to the exam task on page 27.

Question 6: Did you put all your names?

Question 7: Did you remember to put your country? Did you use a capital letter at the beginning?

Question 8: Did you put the day, month and year?

Question 9: Did you put female / F or male / M?

Questions 10 and 11: Did you write these correctly? Look back at Exercise 2 to check.

Question 12: Did you spell this correctly or did you use a number?

Question 13: Did you give a sensible answer?

Question 14: Check that your answer is a kind of fiction book (e.g. a romantic novel, a thriller). You could also write 'none'!

Question 15: Did you sign your name?

▶▶ Exam tip!

You can sometimes write *none* or *nothing* for one of the answers.

▷▷ Extra language practice

1 Vocabulary: books

In the exam you often have to read, write or speak about books.

a) Look at the kinds of books in the box. For each one, decide if it is fiction or non-fiction. Mark *F* or *NF* next to each book. The first one is done for you.

a science fiction story   *F*
a cookery book
a romantic novel
a book about sport
a travel book
a historical novel
a book about animals
a horror story
a history book
a detective story

b) Look at the descriptions below and match each one with one of the books in the box in a).

1 A man tells a woman that he is in love with her.
   a romantic novel
2 It's about a real journey.
3 It describes how a policeman catches a murderer.
4 It gives instructions for how to make a cake.
5 It's a fictional story in the past.
6 It's about the lives of politicians of the past.
7 It's about a group of people living on the moon.
8 Some students are very frightened of a ghost.
9 It's about people who were winners at the Olympic Games.
10 It gives information about lions and tigers.

2 Speaking: guessing

Work with a partner. Can you guess what types of books these are?

Useful language

It could be ...   It's probably ... because ...
I think it might be ...
I don't think it's ... because ...

3 Speaking about books

Work with a partner. Think about a book you have read recently. Ask and answer questions about each other's book. Use these questions to help you.

• What sort of book is it?
• What is it about?
• Why did you choose it?
• What did you like about it?
• What didn't you like about it?

Part 3

> **In Part 3 you have to write a letter.**

 Read the instructions to the exam task below.

1 Who are you going to write to?
2 Why are you writing?
3 The question tells you to write about three things. What are they?
4 How many words must you write?
5 Where must you write your answer?
6 How will the answer begin?

 Plan your answer.

Before starting your letter, it is important to make a plan. This will help you to concentrate on your English when you begin to write. Remember, you have to write about three things.

Look at your answer to question 3 in Exercise 1. Make notes of your ideas for the three parts of the question.

> **▶▶ Exam tip!**
>
> In the exam you can make a plan on the exam paper before you start writing your letter on your answer sheet.

Part 3

Question 16

- An English-speaking friend is coming to visit your town one day next month.
- Now you are writing a letter to tell your friend your plans for the visit.
- Describe where you plan to go, what you will do there and say why you think your friend will enjoy it.
- **Finish the letter on your answer sheet, using about 100 words.**

Dear . . . . . ,

I'm so pleased you are coming to visit my town. ....

....

> You must write your answers on
> the separate answer sheet.

3 ▶ Language focus 1: beginnings and endings

Match the two halves of these six sentences. The first one is done for you.

1 I'm looking forward to ⟍   a) whether you agree with my plans.
2 Let me know   ⟍   b) showing you around my town.
3 It's great   c) you're coming to visit me.
4 Write back soon   d) to hear from you soon.
5 I hope   e) to know you're coming to see me.
6 I'm so pleased that   f) and tell me if you agree with my plans.

Which three sentences can you use at the beginning of a letter? Which three sentences can you use at the end of the letter?

4 ▶ Write your letter.

Look at the notes you made in Exercise 2 on page 29. Think about the language you learnt in Exercise 3. Decide which ending you want to use. Now write your own letter on your answer sheet.

5 ▶ Language focus 2: correcting mistakes

Read the following sentences. Each sentence has two mistakes. Write the correct sentences in your notebook and say what sort of mistakes they are – punctuation, spelling or verb.

1 Every summer my brother and I goes to my grandparents farm for two weeks.
2 There house is built 300 years ago.
3 Its quite large and very beatiful.
4 My brother wants being a farmer when he will finish college.
5 I enjoy to walk in the woods but only when the whether is fine.

6 ▶ Check your letter for mistakes.

Read your letter again and correct any mistakes. Exchange your letter with another student and correct any mistakes you find.

▷▷ Extra language practice

1 ▶ Speaking about an evening out

Work with a partner. An English-speaking friend is going to spend an evening with you both. Decide where you will take him / her and what you will do there. Think about:

• places to eat
• things to do in your town
• things to see

Useful language

Why don't we ...?   How about ...?   We could ... and then we could ...
Yes, that's a good idea.   I am not sure about that.

Example: 'Why don't we go to an Italian restaurant?'

> **Exam tip!**

Before the exam, count 100 words in your usual handwriting so you know what that looks like. Then in the exam it won't be necessary to waste time counting.

> **Key strategy**

Read the instructions and make sure you understand what you have to write about and why. Plan what you will say, then write your answer. Finally, check your answer for any mistakes.

2 ▶ Writing: adding details

It is important to put interesting details in your letter. Here is part of a letter. Read the letter and then look at the phrases in the box. Decide which one fits best in each space. The first one is done for you.

I'm going to take you on a river trip (1) ....e..... . The river goes through the old part of the town, (2) .... After the boat trip we'll have lunch at my favourite restaurant, (3) .... We'll probably see more of my friends there (4) .... I think you'll enjoy your day because you'll meet a lot of people (5) ....

a) which is in a modern shopping centre
b) which has lots of beautiful buildings in it
c) because it's a very popular place with students
d) who I'm sure you'll get on well with
e) with two of my friends

3 ▶ Vocabulary: places to visit

In the exam you often have to write about places to visit and you need to know the names of things you find in them.

Match the words in the box with the places to visit below. Some of the words can go with more than one place.

exhibition gym monkey drawing giraffe locker sculpture elephant cloakroom souvenir book gate showers changing room painting guide ice-cream kiosk net racket postcard fence

art gallery	sports centre	wildlife park
exhibition		

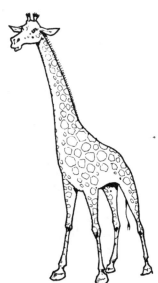

Part 1

> In Part 1 you hear seven different recordings. Sometimes there is one speaker and sometimes there are two.
>
> You listen and choose the correct picture by choosing A, B, C or D.

1 ▸ 🔲 Read and listen to the instructions to the exam task on the opposite page.

1 How many questions are there?
2 How many pictures are there for each question?
3 How many times will you hear each recording?
4 What do you have to do?

▶▶ Exam tip!

At the end of the exam you are given twelve minutes to transfer all your listening answers to the answer sheet. Make sure you copy carefully.

2 ▸ 🔲 Look at the example on the opposite page and listen to the recording.

1 What is the question?
2 What is the answer?
3 How do you know?

3 ▸ Language focus: telling the time

> In Part 1 there is often a question about telling the time. Remember there are different ways to say the time. For example, we can say 'ten thirty-five' or 'twenty-five to eleven'. Both are correct.

How many different ways do you know to say these times?

1   2

3   4

5   6

7 What is another way of saying 12 o'clock in the middle of the night?
8 What is another way of saying 12 o'clock in the middle of the day?
9 What is the difference between 9 a.m. and 9 p.m.?

4 ▸ 🔲 Look at Question 1.

1 What information must you listen for?
2 Look at the four pictures. What are the different ways of saying the times in pictures A, B, C and D?
3 Listen to the recording for Question 1. Which of the times did you hear?
4 Listen again and mark your answer.
5 Why is A wrong?
6 Why is C wrong?
7 Why is D wrong?
8 Why is B the correct answer? What does Paula say?

5 ▸ 🔲 Look at Question 2.

1 What information must you listen for?
2 Look at the four pictures. What words do you think you might hear?
3 Listen to the recording for Question 2 and mark your answer.
4 Listen again and check your answer.

6 ▸ 🔲 Finish the exam task.
Now do Questions 3–7 in the same way.

> ▸ **Key strategy**
> Use the pictures to help you. You can guess a lot about what you are going to hear by looking at them.

Part 1

Questions 1–7

- There are seven questions in this Part.
- For each question there are four pictures and a short recording.
- You will hear each recording twice.
- For each question, look at the pictures and listen to the recording.
- Choose the correct picture and put a tick (✓) in the box below it.

Example: Which train will the woman catch?

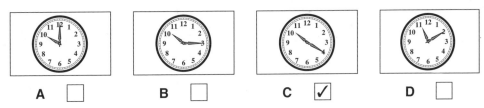

A ☐   B ☐   C ✓   D ☐

1   What time will Paula pick Julie up?

A ☐   B ☐   C ☐   D ☐

2   What will they get first?

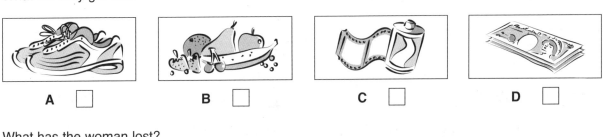

A ☐   B ☐   C ☐   D ☐

3   What has the woman lost?

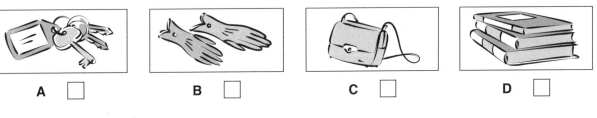

A ☐   B ☐   C ☐   D ☐

4   What will the man eat?

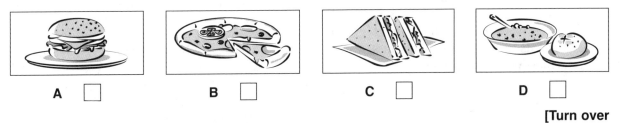

A ☐   B ☐   C ☐   D ☐

[Turn over

5 What time is the woman's new appointment?

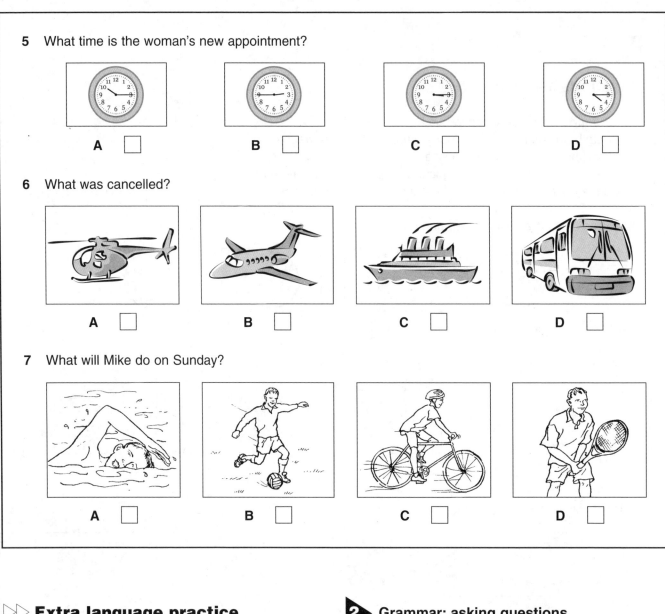

A ☐   B ☐   C ☐   D ☐

6 What was cancelled?

A ☐   B ☐   C ☐   D ☐

7 What will Mike do on Sunday?

A ☐   B ☐   C ☐   D ☐

▷▷ **Extra language practice**

 Vocabulary: word sets

Learning words in groups can help you to remember them. Work with a partner. Arrange the words in the box into groups.

ferry   keys   burger   football   credit cards
sandwich   train   helicopter   bike   pizza
tennis   volleyball   roll   purse   wallet
swimming   coach   soup   diary   cycling

How many other words can you add to each group? Compare your lists with the rest of the class to see who has the most words in each group.

 Grammar: asking questions

In the exam, it is important to know how to make questions and to understand them.

Write questions for these answers in your notebook. The first one is done for you.

1 .*Shall we go swimming*..........................?
Oh, yes. Let's meet at the pool in half an hour.

2 ....?
About one o'clock, usually.

3 ....?
I'd like a sandwich, please.

4 ....?
I missed my bus.

5 ....?
No, I haven't seen them anywhere.

Part 2

> In Part 2 you hear one person speaking. They may be talking to a group of people or on the radio.
>
> You listen and answer the questions by choosing A, B, C or D.

1 Read and listen to the instructions to the exam task below.

1 How many questions are there?
2 Who will you hear?
3 What will she talk about?
4 Who is Robert?
5 Who is Ben?
6 What do you have to do?
7 How many times will you hear the recording?

2 Pronunciation focus: word stress

> If you know how to pronounce a word correctly, you are more likely to understand it when you hear it.

Look at these words which you will hear in Vanessa's talk. Look at the words, say them aloud and mark the main stress.

Example: dec<u>i</u>ded

1 anxious
2 medicines
3 expected
4 considered
5 wonderful
6 preferred
7 dangerous
8 particular
9 together

Part 2

Questions 8–13

- Look at the questions for this Part.
- You will hear a woman, Vanessa, talking about a journey she made with her husband, Robert, and her baby, Ben.
- Put a tick (✓) in the correct box for each question.

---

3 Look at the exam task on the next page and make guesses.

Which of the following do you think the woman will talk about? Put a tick next to them.

- her husband
- a boat
- her baby
- the weather
- how much the journey cost
- what she is doing now
- where they stopped
- Robert's father
- meeting other families
- how long the journey took

▶▶ **Exam tip!**

Some of the wrong answers may seem right because they contain words you hear in the recording.

4 Listen to the recording.
The questions always follow the same order as what you hear on the recording.

1 Look at Question 8. Listen to what Vanessa says about last year and tick the correct answer.
2 Look at Question 9. Listen to what Vanessa was worried about. Be careful – she uses a different word which means the same as worried. Tick the correct answer.
3 Now do Questions 10–13 in the same way. Don't worry if you don't get the answers the first time. You will hear the recording again.

Key strategy

Use the questions to help you understand the recording. The second time you listen, check your answers and answer those that you missed the first time.

8 What did Vanessa and Robert decide to do last year?

A ☐ get married

B ☐ work in Hong Kong

C ☐ travel to England by boat

D ☐ look for new jobs

9 Vanessa was worried that

A ☐ they wouldn't be prepared.

B ☐ they wouldn't find a suitable boat.

C ☐ the conditions would be bad.

D ☐ the baby would get ill.

10 How did Vanessa feel when they reached Singapore?

A ☐ She wondered if she should fly home.

B ☐ She was worried about the boat.

C ☐ She was looking forward to the rest of the journey.

D ☐ She enjoyed the break from travelling.

11 Why was Vanessa's father-in-law particularly helpful?

A ☐ He was a good cook.

B ☐ He played with the baby.

C ☐ He did all the washing-up.

D ☐ He helped to sail the boat.

12 Because of spending so much time on the boat, the baby

A ☐ learnt to walk late.

B ☐ doesn't play by himself.

C ☐ doesn't like climbing.

D ☐ only likes certain food.

13 What is Vanessa's advice for people sailing with children?

A ☐ Don't take more than one child.

B ☐ Go for a short time.

C ☐ Don't let children get bored.

D ☐ Plan the route carefully.

5 Listen to the recording again.

Check the answers you have marked and try to do any you missed the first time. If you still don't know, guess! Do not leave any questions unanswered.

▷▷ **Extra language practice**

1▶ **Vocabulary: adjectives**

Vanessa said '*six boring weeks*' and '*bored children*'. There are several adjective pairs like this. It's important that you understand and use them correctly.

For each sentence, underline the word which fits the space. The first one is done for you.

1 My little sister gets .... if she hasn't got anyone to play with. (<u>bored</u> / boring)
2 It can be very .... to speak a foreign language for a long time. (tired / tiring)
3 I was .... to see so many people in that terrible restaurant. (surprised / surprising)
4 My uncle can do some .... magic tricks. (amazed / amazing)
5 For an adventure film it wasn't very .... (excited / exciting)
6 I was so .... in what I was reading that I forgot to have lunch.
   (interested / interesting)

2▶ **Speaking about a journey**

Work with a partner. Tell your partner about a journey. It can be a real journey you have made or you can invent one.

• Where did you go? (To an island? To the mountains? To a foreign city?)
• How did you get there? (By train? By plane? By car? By boat?)
• Now say what was good and bad about your journey.

Use the language in the box below to help you. After listening to you, your partner must decide if the journey was real or invented.

Useful language
We / I planned ...   I went to ... because I wanted ...   We travelled by ...
I was very surprised by ...   The most interesting thing was ...
I was amazed by ...   ... was very exciting.   ... was a little boring.

3▶ **Grammar: verbs followed by *to do***

Vanessa said '*We decided to sail ...*'. Many verbs in English can be followed by the *to* form of a verb.

Complete these sentences with a suitable verb. The first one is done for you.

1 We decided to .*to sail*. to England last year.
2 My brother expects .... his exams because he's worked hard.
3 I learnt .... in the sea when I was ten.
4 We wanted .... that new film but the queues were too long.
5 My father hopes .... when he is sixty.
6 I planned .... tennis at the weekend but I had too much homework.
7 He promised .... me mend my bicycle if I cleaned his car.
8 If she offers .... her violin to you, find an excuse to leave!
9 We had intended .... him the truth, but we weren't brave enough.

> In Part 3 you hear one person speaking. He or she gives information to a group of
> people or on the radio.
>
> You read some notes and fill in missing information.

1 Read and listen to the instructions to the exam task on the opposite page.

1   How many questions are there?
2   What sort of word is Shipton? How do you know?
3   Who will you hear? What will he talk about?
4   What do you have to do?
5   How many times will you hear the recording?

2 Language focus: guessing the missing word

In Part 3, it is important to guess what kind of word is missing. You can do this by
looking at the words around the numbered spaces. These words can tell you what
kind of word you need to write – noun, verb, adjective, preposition, number, date, etc.

Look at these notes about a museum. Think of the kinds of words or numbers which
might fit the spaces. Don't try to guess exactly what the missing word is, but guess
what kind of word it is. Choose from a) – n) below. The first two are done for you.

BRIDGENORTH MUSEUM

First opened in (**1**) ....*a*.... .
(**2**) ....*f*.... people visit it every year.
Closed in the (**3**) .... from October to (**4**) ....
Restaurant: on the (**5**) .... floor, open from 11 until (**6**) .... every day except (**7**) ....
Shop is (**8**) .... the main exhibition hall.
Special exhibition of (**9**) .... starts on (**10**) .... September.
For guided tours meet in the (**11**) ....
All guides wear (**12**) .... jackets.
Special courses for the public on Thursdays and Fridays.
This week's activity is (**13**) ....
Don't forget to wear (**14**) ....

---

a) a year
b) a day of the week
c) a colour
d) something you can wear
e) a preposition of place
f) a number
g) a season

h) something people can do
i) a level in a building
j) a date
k) a time
l) a month
m) the name of a room
n) something people look at

When you have finished, look at Exercise 1 on page 40 to see if you are right.

3 Look at the exam task below and guess what kind of words are missing.

1 Look at Questions 14, 15, 16 and 17. What kind of word can go in the space. How do you know?
2 Look at Question 18. What kind of information do you need here? How do you know?
3 Look at Question 19. What kind of word can go here? How do you know?

4 Listen to the recording.
   Try to answer as many questions as you can. If you miss a gap, don't worry. You can fill it in the second time you listen.

5 Listen to the recording again.
   Check the answers you wrote the first time. Fill in any answers you missed.

6 Check your answers.

1 How many words did you write in each space?
2 Is the meaning correct?
3 Is the grammar correct?
4 Is the spelling correct?

Part 3

Questions 14–19

- Look at the notes about the Shipton Museum.
- Some information is missing.
- You will hear a man talking on the radio about the museum.
- For each question, fill in the missing information in the numbered space.

Shipton museum

The museum is:
– in a building which was a (**14**) ....
– near the (**15**) .... outside the town.

In the museum, visit:
– a 19th-century (**16**) ....
– a 1950s living room
– an exhibition about (**17**) .... which will
   open on (**18**) ....

To get there:
follow the (**19**) .... signs from the town centre.

Extra language practice

 Speaking about a visit to a museum

Look at these notes about Bridgenorth Museum.
Work with a partner.

Bridgenorth Museum

First opened in 1935.
20,000 visitors every year.

Restaurant: on the first floor, open from
11 until 4.30 every day except Monday.
Shop: next to the main exhibition hall.
Special exhibition of garden sculpture starts on
20th September.

For guided tours meet in the library. All guides
wear blue jackets.

Special courses for the public on Thursdays
and Fridays. This week's activity is making
pots. Don't forget to wear old clothes.

Student A: You are going to visit Bridgenorth Museum
next week. Persuade your partner to come with you.

Student B: Your partner wants you to visit
Bridgenorth Museum with him / her next week. Ask
questions about where it is, what is in it and how to
get there.

Useful language

A	Why don't we ...? There is / are ... You can learn about ...	B	Can we ... there? When ...? What time ...?

 Vocabulary: making adjectives from verbs

> The man you heard on the recording talked about 'a
> 1950s living room'. Many English adjectives are
> made from verbs in this way.

Make an -*ing* adjective from each of the verbs in the
following box. (Be careful about spelling!) Choose
which adjective fits each of the spaces in the
sentences 1–11.

book   dive   drive   fry   run   sleep   swim   ~~wait~~   walk   wash   write

1   We waited for half an hour in the .*waiting*.
room.
2   I usually wash my clothes in the ....
machine.
3   My sister passed her .... test last week.
4   Don't forget your .... costume when you go to
the seaside.
5   We can cook the sausages in this .... pan.
6   I need to buy some .... shoes before I can
go jogging.
7   I wrote to my grandmother on my new ....
paper.
8   Do you have a .... bag for when we go
camping?
9   Did you phone the .... office about our
theatre tickets?
10 The swimmer stood on the .... board, then
jumped into the water.
11 My father is using a .... stick because he has
a bad knee.

 Grammar: prepositions

> In Part 3, prepositions can often help you to decide
> what sort of word can go in a gap, so it's important
> to get lots of practice in understanding and using
> them correctly.

Underline the correct word for each gap. The first one
is done for you.

Shipton Cinema is (**1**) .... (<u>in</u> / on) the new
shopping centre. Cars are not allowed (**2**) ....
(into / to) the centre so it is very pleasant to walk
(**3**) .... (above / around). There are several cafés
where you can buy a snack (**4**) .... (in / on) the
way to the cinema. If you come by car, there is a car
park just (**5**) .... (next / outside) the shopping
centre. You can also catch a bus (**6**) .... (from / in)
the bus stop (**7**) .... (in / of) the main square. It is
easy to find the cinema because there is a big sign in
front (**8**) .... (of / from) it. You can buy tickets by
phone or from the box office which is open every
weekday (**9**) .... (under / until) 10 p.m. It closes
later (**10**) .... (on / in) Saturdays and Sundays.

> In Part 4 you hear two people having a conversation and you read some statements. You must decide whether each statement is correct or incorrect.

1 Read and listen to the instructions to the exam task below.

1 How many statements are there?
2 How many people will you hear?
3 What is the boy's name?
4 What is the girl's name?
5 Where are they?
6 What do you have to do?
7 How many times will you hear the recording?

Remember, at the end of the exam you are given 12 minutes to transfer all your listening answers to the answer sheet. Make sure you copy carefully.

Part 4

Questions 20–25

- Look at the six statements for this Part.
- You will hear a conversation between a boy, William, and a girl, Sophie in a music shop.
- Decide if you think each statement is correct or incorrect.
- If you think it is correct, put a tick (✓) in the box under **A** for **YES**. If you think it is not correct, put a tick (✓) in the box under **B** for **NO**.

2 Language focus: reporting feelings and opinions

In Part 4 you hear people talking about their feelings and opinions.

Use one of the verbs in the box to complete the second sentence so it means the same as the first. The first one is done for you.

| feels | thinks | ~~enjoys~~ | is disappointed | suggests |
| persuade | is keen | refuses | recommends | offers |

1 'I really like shopping for clothes.'
   She .*enjoys*. shopping for clothes very much.

2 'I'm sure I'll win the race this year.'
   He .... confident about winning the race this year.

3 'You really should come with us this evening.'
   They try to .... her to come with them.

4 'I won't lend you any money.'
   He .... to lend her any money.

5 'Shall I help you wash up?'
   He .... to help her wash up.

6 'Why don't we take a holiday next week?'
   She .... taking a holiday next week.

7 'In my opinion, this journey is a waste of time.'
   He .... the journey is a waste of time.

8 'I really want to try wind-surfing while I'm here.'
   She .... to try wind-surfing while she's here.

9 'These peaches are excellent.'
   He .... the peaches.

10 'I hoped to go sailing this weekend but the weather is bad.'
   She .... that she can't go sailing.

3 ▶ Look at the exam task below and make guesses.

Underline six words or phrases which tell you what William and Sophie's conversation will be about. Compare your list of words with another student.

▶▶ **Exam tip!**

The instructions tell you the names of the people and who they are. Make sure you know which speaker is which as this is important for answering the questions.

4 ▶ 🖭 Listen to the recording and answer the questions.

If you miss one, don't worry. You can listen for the answer when you hear the recording again.

5 ▶ 🖭 Listen to the recording again and check your answers.

Try to fill in any you missed the first time. If you still don't know, guess! Do not leave any questions unanswered.

▶ **Key strategy**

Try to read the statements as you listen, but the words you hear may not be exactly the same as the words in the statements.

		A YES	B NO
20	Sophie's mother works in the town where she lives.	☐	☐
21	Sophie enjoys shopping in Birmingham.	☐	☐
22	William feels confident about finding his way around Birmingham.	☐	☐
23	Sophie thinks the band 521 has improved.	☐	☐
24	William persuades Sophie to buy a different CD from him.	☐	☐
		☐	☐

▷▷ Extra language practice

▶ 1 Vocabulary: music

a) Choose the correct word from the box to complete the descriptions of the pictures below.

classical   jazz   pop

1

a .... group

2

a .... orchestra

3

a .... band

b) Can you name the following things?

▶ 2 Speaking: choosing a birthday present

Work with a partner. Imagine you are in a music shop together. You are buying a CD or cassette for a friend's birthday present. Decide what to buy. Talk about the sort of music he / she prefers and what he / she will play it on.

Useful language

What sort of music does he / she like best?
Has he / she got a CD player?
What's his / her favourite group / singer?
Does he / she listen to ...?

▶ 3 Grammar: *if* (unreal situations)

Look at these sentences from William and Sophie's conversation. They are imagining how they'd manage if they went to Birmingham together.

'If we had a map, it wouldn't be a problem for me.'
'If we were together, it would be OK.'

Use your imagination and finish the sentences below in your notebook.

1 If I had lots of money, ...
2 If I were a film star, ...
3 If I were extremely good-looking, ...
4 If I met a famous pop star, ...
5 If I had a private plane, ...
6 If I spoke perfect English, ...
7 If my friends gave a party for me, ...

Part 1

> In the Speaking Test you work with another student.
>
> In Part 1 you ask and answer questions together.
>
> This part lasts 2–3 minutes.
>
> The examiner will ask you to spell a word.

▶ 1   Speaking: asking for and giving personal information

> In Part 1 you have to give information about yourself.

a) Think about meeting new people, for example, when you go on holiday. What do you like to find out about people? Write five questions you might ask in your notebook.

b) Look at the questions below. Are they similar to the questions you wrote? Match the questions (1–7) to the answers (a–g). The first one is done for you.

1 What's your name?   *g*
2 Where do you live?
3 What part of the country is that in?
4 How long have you lived there?
5 What's the name of your school?
6 Do you have any brothers and sisters?
7 Do you have a job?

a) About five years.
b) It's called Manchester Grammar School
c) Yes, one sister. She's older than me.
d) In the north.
e) In Manchester.
f) Well not really. But I work in a café sometimes during the holidays.
g) John Brown.

Look carefully at the answers. Are they all complete sentences? Which give extra information?

c) Work with a partner. Ask each other the questions in b) above. Try to give some extra information for questions 6 and 7. When you have finished, write the answers you gave in your notebook.

▶▶ Exam tip!

It is important to ask questions clearly so that your partner can understand them.

▶ 2   Pronunciation focus: questions

a) Look at these questions and listen to the recording. Which ones go up at the end (↗) and which ones go down (↘)? Mark them with arrows. The first one is done for you.

1 Where is your school?
2 What's your best subject?
3 Do you like sport?
4 How long is your holiday?
5 Are you going to the seaside?
6 Have you ever been to Mexico?

Listen again and check your answers.

b) Look at the questions in Exercise 1 again. Which ones go up at the end (↗) and which ones go down (↘)? Mark them with arrows. Listen to the recording and repeat the questions.

▶ 3   Language focus: spelling

> In Part 1, it is important for you to know the alphabet in English as you will be asked to spell something.

a) What are the names of these letters?

A   C   E   G   H   I   J   K   Q   R   S   U   V   W   X   Y   Z

b) What do you say when a letter is repeated, for example the *m* in *grammar*?

c) Work with a partner. One of you is going to write, and the other is going to speak.

Student A: Look at page 50.

Student B: Write down what your partner says in your notebook. When you have finished, show your words to Student A. Are they spelt correctly?

Now change roles.

Student B: Spell the names of the following cities for your partner.
1 Tokyo
2 Cairo
3 Rio de Janeiro
4 Teheran
5 Marseilles

d) Now spell the names of the cities and streets where you both live. Write them in your notebooks and then check them.

4 ▶ Look at the exam task below.
Work with a different partner.

> You imagine you don't know each other. The examiner tells you to ask each other questions to find out some information about each other. Close your books and ask each other at least four of the questions you have practised.
> Also, ask each other a spelling question.
> Example: *'Siv, you said you live in Stockholm – how do you spell that?'*

5 ▶ **Sample interview**

a) Listen to a recording of Part 1. Which of the questions below do Paolo and Marta ask each other? Tick the ones you hear.

1 What's your name?
2 Where do you live?
3 Which part of London is that in?
4 How long have you lived there?
5 What is the name of your school?
6 Do you have any brothers and sisters?
7 Do you have a job?

b) Listen again.

1 Do Paolo and Marta give any extra information?
2 What does Paolo say when he doesn't understand?

6 ▶ **Language practice: correcting mistakes**

Look at this conversation between Maria and José.
Can you correct their mistakes?

1 (What's you name?)
2 (I called José.)
3 (Where you live?)
4 (At Malaga.)
5 (What part the country is that in?)
6 (In south.)
7 (How long time have you lived there?)
8 (About six month.)

Part 2

> In Part 2 the examiner gives you and your partner some pictures to look at.
> You talk about them together.

1 ▶ **Speaking: asking for and giving information**

a) You need to find out about a place before you visit it. What questions will you ask to get the following information? Write the questions in your notebook.

Example:
what it's called   *What is it called?*

1 where it is
2 how you can get there
3 what you can see or do there
4 what time it opens / closes
5 how much it costs to go in

b) Work with a partner.

Student A: Look at the information about a shopping mall called the Grafton Centre on page 50.

Student B: Your partner has some information about a shopping mall. Do you want to visit it? Ask questions to find out about it.

2 ▶ **Speaking: making plans**

a) Look at the following sentences (1–12) and match them with the descriptions (a–e) below. The first one is done for you.

1 Let's go to   *b*
2 All right, let's do it!
3 What do you want to do?
4 Right. We'll do that.
5 How about going to ...?
6 Shall we go to ...?
7 Where would you prefer to go?
8 That sounds good. Let's do that.
9 I'm not so sure about that.
10 Sure. I'd like to do that.
11 That's a great idea.
12 Can we try something else?

a) finding out what your partner wants to do
b) making a suggestion
c) agreeing with a suggestion
d) disagreeing
e) agreeing that a decision has been made

b) Read the following conversation between Kai and Noriko who are planning their day. Fill each space with a suitable word.

Kai: Let's plan our day.
Noriko: OK. Where shall we (**1**) .go. first?
Kai: How (**2**) .... going to look round the market?
Noriko: What can we (**3**) .... there?
Kai: We might buy a few souvenirs.
Noriko: I'm not so (**4**) .... about that. If we buy anything, we'll have to carry it all day.
Kai: That's true. So where (**5**) .... you like to go first?
Noriko: What (**6**) .... the museum?
Kai: Well, what can we (**7**) .... there?
Noriko: They have lots of great paintings there.
Kai: OK. And what (**8**) .... we do after that?
Noriko: (**9**) .... go somewhere for lunch.
Kai: That's a great (**10**) .... Where shall we go?
Noriko: Shall we go for a pizza?
Kai: Sure. I'd (**11**) .... to do that. And what shall we do after lunch?
Noriko: Well, then we could go to the market.
Kai: All right. (**12**) .... do it!
Noriko: OK. I'm ready.

Work with a partner. One of you will be Kai, the other, Noriko. Read the conversation aloud.

c) Work with a partner. Plan an afternoon when you are going to visit The Grafton Centre. Use the language you have been practising in a) and b).

 3 **Vocabulary: places of interest**

What kinds of things can you see in these places? Write down four for each. Compare your list with another student.

1 a museum
2 a zoo
3 a garden
4 a house
5 a market

 Key strategy
Listen carefully to what your partner says, so that you can give a suitable answer, like people having a real conversation.

 4 Look at the exam task below. Work with a partner.

You are going to make plans for a day out. Look at page 147. There are some pictures of places to visit. Decide together which **three** places you are going to go to. Decide which you will go to first. Ask and answer questions like these:
- Which places would you like to go to?
- What about …?
- Where would you like to go first?
- Why?
- What shall we do after that?

 **Exam tip!**

If you are not sure what to do, ask the examiner to repeat the instructions.

5 📼 **Sample interview**

a) Listen to a recording of Part 2 and look at the picture on page 147. Which places do Paolo and Marta decide to go to?

b) Listen again. Which of the expressions below do Paolo and Marta use? Tick the ones you hear.

1 What do you want to do?
2 Right, we'll do that.
3 Shall we go to …?
4 That sounds good. Let's do that.
5 Can we try something else?
6 Where would you like to go?
7 Let's go to …
8 How about going to …?
9 Right, we'll do that.
10 That's a great idea.
11 Sure, I'd like to do that.
12 All right, let's do that!

Part 3

> In Part 3 the examiner gives you and your partner a photograph each.
> You talk about your photograph to your partner.

1 ▶ Speaking: describing where people and things are in a picture

a) Label the picture below, using the phrases in the box.

| in the distance   behind the dancers   beside the audience   in the middle
| in front of the dancers |

b) Work with a partner. Take turns to ask each other where things are in this picture.

2 ▶ Vocabulary: describing people

> In Part 3 you will often have to describe people and their clothes.

Look at what Sara writes about herself:

I'm fairly tall and quite fat. My hair is dark. It's straight and fairly short. I don't wear glasses.

a) Work with a partner. Write down the names of six famous people. Take turns to describe one of them. Talk about their size and their hair. Say whether they wear glasses. Try to guess who your partner is describing. Use the words in the boxes to help you.

Size:

He / She is	quite rather very extremely	tall. short. slim. fat. thin.
	average size.	

Hair:

His / Her hair is	rather fairly very	curly. straight. long. short.
	red / black / dark / fair / blond.	

b) Now write three sentences about yourself in your notebook.

3 ▶ Vocabulary: clothes

Match the words in the box to the pictures below.

> a pair of jeans   a pair of boots   a pair of shorts
> a pullover   a shirt   a jacket   a belt   a suit
> a T-shirt   a skirt   a dress   a cap   a tie

4 ▶ 🔊 Pronunciation focus: clothes words

a) Which of the words in the box below have the same vowel sounds in them? Put them in four pairs.

Example: shirt, skirt

> ~~shirt~~   boots   belt   cap   dress   suit
> ~~skirt~~   jacket

b) Listen to the recording and check your answers.

c) Listen again and repeat the words.

d) Work with a partner. Tell each other what you wore last Saturday.

5 ▶ Writing: describing what people are doing

Work with a partner. Think about the pictures in Exercise 1 but don't look at them. Can you remember what all the people are doing in each of the pictures?

Example:
In picture 1, some people are sitting on the ground.

When you have finished, look at the pictures to see if you have forgotten anything.

Key strategy

Remember to say what is happening in your photograph as well as what things there are in it.

6 Look at the exam task below. Work with a partner.

> Candidate A: look at photograph 1A on page 152.
> Candidate B: look at photograph 1B on page 154.
>
> Think about your photograph for a few seconds. Describe it to your partner for about one minute. Tell your partner about these things:
> • the kind of place it is
> • what you can see in different parts of the picture
> • what the people look like
> • what they are wearing
> • what they are doing
> • whether the people look happy or not.

▶▶ Exam tip!

Don't worry if you don't know the name of something – describe it instead.

7 **Sample interview**

a) Listen to a recording of Part 3 and look at the pictures on pages 152 and 154. Which of the expressions below do Paolo and Marta use?

1 in the distance 4 in the middle
2 behind 5 in front of
3 beside

b) Listen again. Do Paolo and Marta talk about the things in the box below. Put a tick (✓) under P for the things that Paolo talks about and under M for the things that Marta talks about.

	P	M
the kind of place it is		
what the people look like		
what they are wearing		
what they are doing		
whether the people look happy or not		

c) How does Paolo explain the word that he doesn't know?

Part 4

> In Part 4 the examiner asks you to talk to your partner about a particular subject.
> You give your opinion about something and explain what you prefer.

1 ▶ **Speaking: likes and dislikes**

Work with a partner. Find out what your partner likes doing on holiday. Use the language in the box to help you. Add two other holiday activities to the list.

> How do you feel about ...?
> I hate / don't like / quite like / love ...

• visiting relatives   • going to theme parks
• shopping   • doing lots of sports
• sunbathing   • going around museums
• visiting old houses   • exploring new places
• being on my own   • spending time with
• staying in hotels   friends

Do you both like / dislike the same things?

2 ▶ **Vocabulary: opposites**

Look at the adjectives in box A. Can you find an opposite for each of the adjectives in box B?

A	~~restful~~ quiet relaxing ordinary cheap boring

B	unusual expensive ~~active~~ noisy exciting stressful

Example:
restful / active

3 ▶ **Speaking: saying why you like or don't like something**

Look at the activities in Exercise 1 on page 49, and the extra ones you added. Discuss with your partner why he / she likes some activities and why he / she doesn't like others. Use the adjectives in Exercise 2 to explain your answers.

Example:
'Why do / don't you like sunbathing?'
'Because it's relaxing / boring.'

 ▶▶ **Exam tip!**

Listen carefully to what your partner says so you can give a good answer.

 4 ▶ **Writing a postcard**

How well do your classmates know you? Imagine you are on holiday now. On a piece of paper, write a 'postcard' to the class. Say where you are. Tell the class what you like doing and what you don't like doing there. Don't put your name on it.

Put all the 'postcards' in a pile. Take turns to read out someone's card and let the class guess who wrote it.

▶ **Key strategy**

It's important to give a reason for your opinions – it makes the conversation much more interesting.

 5 ▶ Look at the exam task below.
Work with a partner.

Tell each other about what you like doing on holiday. Use these ideas.

- Say what kind of places you like to visit
- Say what you do there
- Say what you don't like doing on holiday. Why?

 **6** ▶ **Sample interview**

a) Listen to a recording of Part 4 and look at the activities in the box below. Under M for Marta put a tick (✓) for the activities she enjoys and a cross (✗) for the activities she doesn't enjoy. Do the same for Paolo.

	M	P
watersports		
visiting old houses		
swimming		
sitting on the beach		
shopping		
doing something quiet		
going to the theatre		
going to restaurants		

b) Listen to the recording again and write down the words Paolo and Marta use to say why they like or don't like something.

c) Compare your answers with your partner.

Example:
'Paolo says he likes doing watersports because they're exciting and Marta says they're fun.'

Speaking Part 1, Exercise 3

Student A: Spell the names of the following cities for your partner.
1 Venice
2 Athens
3 Barcelona
4 Buenos Aires
5 Vienna

Now change roles.

Student A: Write down what your partner says in your notebook. When you have finished, show your words to Student B. Are they spelt correctly?

Speaking Part 2, Exercise 1

Student A: Answer your partner's questions using the information below.

THE GRAFTON CENTRE (10 minutes' walk from city centre)
Many different shops and department stores. Also cafés, fast food and cinema.
Open daily, between 8 a.m. and 9 p.m.

TEST 2

In Test 2 there are more exercises:

- to help you understand how to approach each exam task
- to give you practice in the language you need for the exam.

Grammar checklist

- *if* sentences
- *although*
- *for* and *ago*
- *how often?*
- reported speech
- prepositions
- verbs + *to* or *should*
- comparisons
- possessives
- *get*

Reading

Part 1

> In Part 1 you read signs, notices or labels which you might see in Britain.
> You choose the correct meaning for the signs from four explanations.

 Read the instructions to the exam task on the opposite page.

1 How many questions must you answer?
2 What are the questions about?
3 Where do you mark your answers?

 Look at the example on the opposite page.

1 What is the answer?
2 How is it marked?

▶▶ Exam tip!

Some of the words in the wrong sentences are often the same as in the sign. Don't choose too quickly. Make sure you understand the meaning of the whole sentence before you decide.

 Look at Question 1.
   Find the right answer.

1 Where might you see this sign?
2 What words help you to decide? Underline them.
3 Can 'saver' tickets be used on the 10.15 train?
4 Can you use 'saver' tickets on later trains?
5 How do you know?
6 Can you use 'saver' tickets on earlier trains?
7 Does the sign tell you about the cost of the tickets?
8 Look at A, B, C and D. Which one means the same as the sign?

4 ▶ Language focus: money words

The signs and questions in Part 1 are often about buying things. You need to know words for talking about money, for example, 'Saver tickets *cost extra* if you travel after 10.15'.

Choose a word or phrase from the box to fill each space in the text below. The first one is done for you.

| buy   change   cheap   cheaper   correct money |
| cost extra   credit card   discount   pay   sell |

When you go to London on the train you can
(1) .buy. your ticket at the local station using a
(2) .... Sometimes you can get a
(3) .... ticket, because there is a
(4) .... on the fare at certain times of
the day. Make sure you have plenty of
(5) .... with you, because when you
arrive in London, you can use it to
(6) .... for your underground ticket
from a machine. If you don't have the
(7) ...., you may have to queue at the
ticket office. You can also go to London by coach. This
is (8) .... than the train, although it
takes longer. The driver can (9) ....
you a ticket, and it doesn't (10) .... to
travel at busy times of day.

 Finish the task.
   Look at the other signs (2–5) on the opposite page. Choose the correct answer for each one and mark them on your answer sheet.

> **Key strategy**
>
> *Complete the following:*
>
> **When choosing the correct explanation for each sign, look at each option and decide whether it says the .... as the sign.**
>
> *(If you don't remember, look at page 8.)*

Part 1

Questions 1–5

- Look at the sign in each question.
- Someone asks you what it means.
- Mark the letter next to the correct explanation – **A**, **B**, **C** or **D** – **on your answer sheet**.

Example:

0

> **DO NOT PARK YOUR CAR BY THESE GATES**

A Parking near these gates is forbidden.

B The entrance to the car park is through these gates.

C Do not bring your car into this park.

D Close these gates after parking your car.

Example answer:

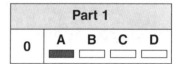

Part 1				
	A	B	C	D
0	■	☐	☐	☐

1

> SAVER TICKETS CAN BE USED ON THE 10.15 TRAIN AND ANY TRAIN AFTER THAT

A The first train you can travel on with a 'saver' ticket is the 10.15.

B 'Saver' tickets cost extra if you travel after 10.15.

C After 10.15 it is not possible to use a 'saver' ticket.

D The 10.15 is the only train you can travel on with a 'saver' ticket.

2

> **THIS MACHINE IS OUT OF ORDER TODAY.**
> **BUY DRINKS AND SNACKS AT THE KIOSK**

A The kiosk is closed today so you will have to use the machine.

B The kiosk has a better choice of drinks and snacks than the machine.

C The machine no longer sells drinks, just snacks.

D Drinks and snacks are only available from the kiosk at present.

[Turn over

3

YOU CAN GET A
50% DISCOUNT
ON SOME GOODS
IF YOU HAVE A
STUDENT CARD

A You can get a student card more cheaply here.

B Half our goods are cheaper for students.

C Students can buy some things at half price.

D Students can buy everything more cheaply here.

4

**THE BUS DRIVER
TAKES CASH ONLY.
THE TICKET OFFICE
TAKES CREDIT
CARDS OR CASH.**

A You need the correct money to pay the bus driver.

B You cannot pay the bus driver with a credit card.

C The ticket office can give you change for the bus.

D It is not possible to buy a ticket with a credit card.

5

TELL THE
RECEPTIONIST
YOUR NAME ON
ARRIVAL, THEN GO
TO THE DENTIST'S
WAITING ROOM

A Do not leave the waiting room until the receptionist calls your name.

B The receptionist will tell you where to wait for the dentist.

C The receptionist will tell the dentist that you have arrived.

D Do not go to the waiting room before telling the receptionist you are here.

Extra language practice

 Grammar: time words and phrases

In Part 1, words and phrases like *after that*, *at present*, *no longer* and *until* can be very important when you are choosing your answer.

Look at these sentences from Part 1.

- *Saver tickets can be used on the 10.15 train and any train **after that**.*
- *Drinks and snacks are only available from the kiosk **at present**.*

Rewrite the sentences below in your notebook using the expressions from the box instead of the words underlined. The first one is done for you.

after that   ~~at present~~   every fifteen minutes
within a fortnight   no longer   until

Example:
The restaurant is not open <u>now</u>.
The restaurant is not open at present.

1 I'm on holiday <u>from now to</u> Tuesday.
2 That film is <u>not</u> showing <u>any more</u>.
3 The museum is closed for lunch, but it will be open <u>afterwards</u>.
4 There's a tram from here to the city centre <u>four times an hour</u>.
5 I promise I'll reply to your request <u>in less than two weeks</u>.

 Vocabulary: number words

Say and write the words for these numbers.

Example:

 three and a half

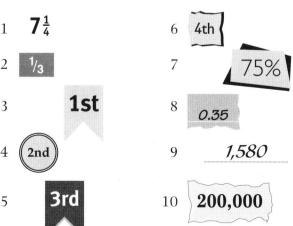

 Grammar: *if* sentences

In the exam you often see sentences with *if* giving information, advice or instructions.

Look at the following sentences.

- *You can get a 50% discount on some goods **if** you have a student card.*
- ***If** there is no one at reception, speak to the security guard.*
- *Please go to customer services on the ground floor **if** you wish to exchange goods.*

Match the two halves of these sentences. The first one is done for you.

1 If you get lost   *c*
2 Tell the security guard
3 If you want to get a discount
4 You may pay less for things
5 Ask an assistant
6 If you're not sure what to buy
7 You should go to a cheaper shop

a) apply to customer services.
b) if you want to save money.
c) meet us at the information desk.
d) if you would like to try something on.
e) if you have a student card.
f) we can help you decide.
g) if your purse is stolen.

Complete the following sentences with your own ideas.

8 Shopping is fun if ....
9 If you can't find what you want in one shop, you ....
10 If a shop assistant is rude to you, ...
11 You can usually return goods to a shop if ....
12 If you want to get a job in a shop, ...

> In Part 2 each question describes different people.
> You match the people to the texts on the opposite page.

 Read the instructions to the task on the opposite page.

1 How many questions are there?
2 What do all the people want?
3 What are the texts about?

4 How many texts are there?
5 What do you have to decide?
6 Where do you mark your answers?

 Look at Questions 6–10 on the opposite page and think about the information given.

Each question describes a different person. Look at the pictures first. Think about the kind of people they show. All the people are looking for something different. For example, in Question 6 we can underline the things which are important for Robert.

---

6    Robert prefers to watch <u>old-fashioned comedy films</u> on TV particularly those with <u>famous actors</u>. He is <u>not</u> keen on <u>musicals or thrillers</u>.

Now underline the important parts of Questions 7–10.

 Language focus: similar meanings

In Part 2 you need to understand when different words or phrases have similar meanings, for example someone may say 'I like stories from literature' or 'I enjoy great novels'.

The phrases below on the left are from Questions 6–10. Match them to the phrases with similar meanings on the right. The first one is done for you.

1 old-fashioned film
2 musical
3 thriller
4 romantic film
5 comedy film
6 in real life
7 well-known stars

a) funny film
b) famous actors
c) film with singing
d) love story
e) this actually happened
f) adventure film
g) film made in the past

Part 2

Questions 6–10

- The people below all want to watch a film on TV.
- On the next page there are descriptions of eight films.
- Decide which film (**letters A–H**) would be the most suitable for each person (**numbers 6–10**).
- For each of these numbers mark the correct letter **on your answer sheet**.

Example answer:

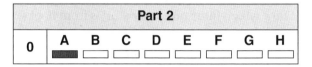

Part 2								
0	A	B	C	D	E	F	G	H

6   Robert prefers to watch old-fashioned comedy films on TV particularly those with famous actors. He is not keen on musicals or thrillers.

7   Simon loves reading. His favourite books are those by famous authors of the past, and he enjoys watching films on TV whose stories are taken from literature. He reads books about the cinema too and likes watching famous actors.

8   Paula likes to relax by watching the latest romantic films on TV especially if they make her laugh. She particularly likes those which have some music in them.

9   Rosie enjoys watching thrillers which are about adventures which actually happened to people in real life as she is interested in the lives of other people.

10   Suzanna's hobby is listening to pop music and reading music magazines. She enjoys watching anything new about pop stars or their music and doesn't mind what sort of film it is.

4 ► Look at the texts below.

1 Look at Question 6 again. Robert prefers to watch comedy films. Mark which films are funny.
2 Which texts do you need to read carefully?
3 Which of the films are old-fashioned?
4 Are either of these films musicals or thrillers?
5 So, which is the best film for Robert?
6 Mark the letter (A, B, C, etc.) by Question 6 on your answer sheet.
7 Now look at Question 7. Simon enjoys watching films whose stories are taken from literature. Mark which films take their stories from books. Read those texts carefully.
8 Which is the best film for Simon?
9 Check your answer. Does it have famous actors? Is the story set in the past?
10 Mark the letter (A, B, C, etc.) by Question 7 on your answer sheet.

► ► **Exam tip!**

Remember there are eight texts and only five people so three texts are not needed.

5 ► Finish the exam task.
Look at the important points you underlined for Questions 8–10. Use them to help you decide which films are the most suitable for the other people. Then mark your answers on your answer sheet.

► **Key strategy**

Complete the following:

.... the important points in the questions before you start so you don't waste time reading through the .... texts.

(If you don't remember, look at page 12.)

This week's TV films reviewed by Jonathan Black

A **See you in San Francisco**

This is a musical comedy made in the 1950s. It's about a journey across the USA in the 1950s. Some young people travel across the USA in an old bus but nothing really exciting happened to them and it isn't actually very funny. I had never heard of the actors although some of them could certainly sing.

B **Tell me again**

This follows the usual story – boy meets girl, they fall in love and sing some songs about it. Although there's nothing special about the singing, it's an enjoyable film and it has its amusing parts. It was only made last year so comes to the TV screen very quickly.

C **Sing it again**

Everyone's queuing to see this film since it came out last month. The music of this group, *Five Alive*, is very popular with young people and so there will be a whole generation of fans watching.

D **On Windermere**

Beautifully filmed, this film keeps perfectly to the novel by Charlotte Raven written two hundred years ago. I got bored by the dialogue which seems so slow compared to modern films but this will be very popular with lovers of Raven's writing. The main roles are all acted by well-known stars of film or TV.

E **Wish you were here**

I first saw this film 25 years ago and it is still as funny as it was then. It is set in a seaside hotel which has lots of problems and some very strange guests. The main actors were already well known when it was made and went on to make several more films together.

F **Route to freedom**

Virginia Timms is a journalist who was a prisoner for a year in one of the most dangerous parts of the world. She had planned to stay only six weeks and this adventure film tells how she escaped from the people who held her. It is difficult to believe that this actually happened to someone who is still alive.

G **Across the universe**

This is one of several very similar films made recently about adventures in space. It's one of the better ones as it certainly holds your attention. But I'm afraid I wanted to laugh sometimes although it isn't supposed to be funny.

H **Beyond the hill**

If you've read William Shore's book of the same name you'll be pleased to watch this beautiful film. If you haven't read it you'll still enjoy this film with excellent acting from some completely unknown actors. It shows the problems of a family in Britain today without making us feel depressed.

Extra language practice

 Speaking about films

Think about a film you have enjoyed.

- What kind of film is it?
- What happens in it?

Work with a partner. Don't tell each other the name of the film you are thinking about! Tell your partner what kind of film it is and describe what happens in it. Say why you like it so much.

Try to guess the name of the film your partner is describing. Do you both like the same types of films?

Useful language

This film is about ...
The best part of the film is when ...
It's one of my favourite films because ...

 Grammar: *although*

> You will often meet sentences which contain the word *although* in the exam. Understanding how this word works will help you make sense of these sentences.

Look at these sentences from the text.

- *I had never heard of the actors **although** some of them could certainly sing.*
- ***Although** there's nothing special about the singing, it's an enjoyable film.*

Complete the sentences (1–6) with one of the phrases below (a–f). The first one is done for you.

1 Although ....*e*...., he doesn't earn very much money.
2 I don't enjoy pop music although ....
3 My brother passed all his exams although ....
4 Although ...., we won the match.
5 Although ...., I haven't lost any weight.
6 I couldn't find a coat I liked, although ....

a) I went to every shop in town
b) we were extremely tired
c) he did very little work
d) I've been on a diet
e) he works very hard
f) most of my friends like it

Grammar: *for* and *ago*

- We use *ago* to talk about when something happened in the past:
  *I first saw this film twenty-five years **ago**.*
  This answers the question: *When did you first see this film?*

- We use *for* to talk about a period of time:
  *She was a prisoner **for** a year.*
  This answers the question: *How long was she a prisoner?*

Complete the answers to these questions in your notebook, using *for* or *ago* and the words in brackets.

Example:
When did you meet your new boyfriend? (six weeks)
I met him .*six weeks ago*..

1 How long were you in New York? (three days)
  We were there ....

2 When were these sandwiches made?
  (half an hour)
  They were made ....

3 How long was your brother in hospital? (two days)
  He was ....

4 How long did you sleep last night? (seven hours)
  I ....

5 When did your grandparents get married?
  (nearly fifty years)
  My ....

6 When did you start working there? (ten years)
  I ....

7 How long was she at the holiday camp?
  (two weeks)
  She ....

8 When did the football match finish? (ten minutes)
  It ....

Part 3

> In Part 3 there are some statements about a text.
> You read the text and decide whether the statements are true or false.

1 Read the instructions to the exam task on the opposite page.

1 How many statements are there?
2 What are the statements about?
3 What do you have to read?
4 What do you have to decide?
5 When do you mark *A* on your answer sheet?
6 When do you mark *B* on your answer sheet?

2 Read statements 11–20 to get a good idea what the text is about.
Find which statement is about each of the following topics and write the number next to it. The first one is done for you.

a) buying food   *16*
b) learning a new sport
c) who should read this
d) the opening times of an office
e) something which gives information about accommodation
f) singing or playing for an audience
g) improving your skill in a leisure activity
h) something many people want to do
i) something which helps you to spend less money
j) who you can ask about something

3 Now read the text on the opposite page.
For each of the ten statements, mark on the text where you think the answer is.

▶▶ Exam tip!

The questions are in the same order as the information you need in the text.

4 Language focus: student life

> In the exam you often need to understand or use words about student life.

The words in the box are used in the statements and text. Match them with the explanations below. The first one is done for you.

> advanced   canteen   club   full-time course
> hostel   noticeboard   part-time course
> reading list   rent   sports centre   student card
> ~~university term~~   welfare office

1 part of the students' year   *university term*
2 money paid to your landlord
3 a place where students can go for general help and advice
4 something you can use to prove that you are a student
5 a place to eat
6 a group who join together for a leisure activity
7 studying for a few hours every week
8 studying all day, from Monday to Friday
9 a place for students to live cheaply
10 the books that students must read for their course
11 where you can play volleyball, do gymnastics, etc.
12 where people put posters and other information
13 a word to describe students who know a lot about their subject

5 Finish the exam task.
Look at each statement again, find the right part of the text and decide whether the statement is correct or incorrect. Mark your answer on your answer sheet.

> ## Key strategy
>
> *Complete the following:*
> **Read the statements before you read the text. Mark the parts of the text which contain the .... you need.**
> *(If you don't remember, look at page 14.)*

Part 3

Questions 11–20

- Look at the statements about advice for new students at a university.
- Read the text below to decide if each statement is correct or incorrect.
- If it is correct, mark **A on your answer sheet**.
- If it is incorrect, mark **B on your answer sheet**.

Example answer:

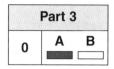

11   This information is to help students who have arrived after the start of the university term.

12   The Welfare Office is usually closed in the morning.

13   A list of flats available for rent can be seen in the Welfare Office.

14   You can save money on books if you have a student card.

15   You should ask older students for advice about where to buy books.

16   Having all your meals in the canteen is the cheapest way to eat.

17   Lots of students want to join the cookery class.

18   You can take up golf at a local club.

19   You can join a part-time course at the Music School if you already play reasonably well.

20   At musical open evenings you can perform even if you have no experience.

NEW STUDENTS' NEWSLETTER 19th September

WELCOME!

As a new student, you've arrived two days before term starts to look around and get settled in before your course begins and the place fills up. Here is some information to make all that a bit easier (we hope!).

The Student Welfare Office is normally open from 4 p.m. till 8 p.m. Monday to Friday. Today and tomorrow it will be open all day, from about 9 a.m. This is the place to come if you have any problems, for example about money (*not yet, surely?*) or accommodation (we have a list of rental agencies and also advertise any rooms which become available in the university hostels at the end of term). We also give out university identity cards which you need to join the library and which allow you to get discounts at a number of local shops (including bookshops) and places of entertainment, such as clubs and cinemas.

On Monday and Tuesday of next week, second-year students will be running a book sale in the canteen from 10–3. Many of the books on your first-year reading list will be available and we suggest you should look here first before spending too much on new books.

The university canteen (open from 7.30 a.m. till 7.30 p.m.) sells hot meals, fairly cheaply, as well as snacks and drinks, but it'll save you money to cook at least some of your own meals. There is a basic cookery course starting next week (run by students for students, so it's really practical). If you don't know how to boil an egg, this is for you. It's always full, so get your name on the list in the welfare office NOW!

The sports centre is open from today. Look on the noticeboards there for information about athletics, swimming, team games, and so on. It is also possible to join some local city clubs, such as golf or squash, at a discount (show them your card) if you can play at a reasonable level. Addresses in the sports centre office.

The Music School welcomes all members of the university, whatever their main subject of study, for part-time courses. Why not take the opportunity to start learning the guitar, violin or piano while you're here? Many advanced students offer really cheap lessons. There are also open evenings when anyone can take the chance to perform in front of an audience. Look out for notices advertising times and dates.

Extra language practice

 Grammar: *how often?*

Look at this sentence from the text.

*The Student Welfare Office is **normally** open from 4 p.m. till 8 p.m.*

The words in the box are used to show how often something happens.

~~always~~ often frequently regularly sometimes ~~usually~~ normally rarely seldom never

a) **Work with a partner. Complete the diagram below with the words from the box. The first two are done for you.**

How often?

```
100%                    50%                    0%
always usually
```

b) **Complete each of these sentences as truthfully as you can, using one of the words from the box.**

1 I .... arrive late for class.
2 I .... have problems with my homework.
3 Our teacher .... speaks English in the classroom.
4 My classmates and I .... meet at weekends.
5 We .... compare our answers to grammar exercises.
6 My friends .... help me with words I don't understand.
7 I .... have to explain some English for my friends.
8 We .... eat English food.
9 My family .... goes abroad for holidays.
10 I .... use an English dictionary to check words I don't know.

 Speaking: *how often?*

Work with a partner. Tell each other how often you do the following activities. Use the words from Exercise 1. Ask: *How often do you ...?*

go jogging   drive a car   play football use a computer   visit art galleries go to the cinema   do the washing-up go to bed after midnight   get up after midday

 Grammar: longer sentences

Understanding how short sentences can be joined to make longer ones is useful for the exam.

Look at the following sentences. They are made from two shorter ones.

• *We also give out university identity cards **which** you need to join the library.*
  = *We also give out university identity cards. + You need **the cards** to join the library.*

• *Students will be running a book sale in the canteen **where** many of the books on your reading list will be available.*
  = *Students will be running a book sale in the canteen. + Many of the books on your reading list will be available **at the sale**.*

• *There are also open evenings **when** anyone can take the chance to perform.*
  = *There are also open evenings. + Anyone can take the chance to perform **on those evenings**.*

Make longer sentences by joining these pairs. Use *which* (for things), *where* (for places) or *when* (for times) to replace the words underlined.

Example:
I've got two good dictionaries. You can borrow <u>my dictionaries</u> if you like.
I've got two good dictionaries which you can borrow if you like.

1 We're going to the university swimming pool. International competitions take place <u>at the pool</u>.
2 I like to go jogging early in the morning. The air is clean <u>early in the morning</u>.
3 I usually study in the college library. Most of my friends study <u>in the college library</u> too.
4 It's a pity we have exams in the summer. The weather is very hot <u>in the summer</u>.
5 We're studying for a test. Our teacher is giving us <u>the test</u> soon.

Part 4

In Part 4 you read a text.

You then answer some questions about it by choosing A, B, C or D.

 1 Read the instructions to the exam task below.

1 What do you have to read?
2 What do you have to do?
3 Where do you mark your answers?

2 Read the text quickly and think about these questions.

1 What sort of place is the text about?
2 Why does the writer enjoy going there?
3 What happened there in 1975?

3 Language focus: attitudes

In the text several people express attitudes. Match the people (a–d) below with the following. Who ...

1 said drowning the village was the best thing that ever happened?
2 never think about the drowned houses?
3 was surprised?
4 still feel angry about what happened?
5 still miss the village?
6 thinks it's a shame?
7 hope something similar never happens again?
8 would miss the watersports?

a) the shop owner
b) the writer of the text
c) people who used to live in Vinnthorpe
d) people doing watersports

Part 4

Questions 21–25

- Read the text and questions below.
- For each question, mark the letter next to the correct answer – **A**, **B**, **C** or **D** – on your answer sheet.

Example answer:

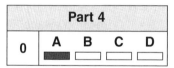

Part 4			
0	A	B	C	D

My favourite place for watersports is Lake Vinney but it has only existed since 1975 when the valley was filled with water to provide electricity. Under the water is the village, Vinnthorpe. Last week I talked to Pat Smithers who runs a shop on the edge of the lake and looks after the huge car park. She said drowning the village was the best thing that ever happened as it brought a lot of business to the area and the number of visitors from all over the country continues to increase. When I asked people enjoying the watersports, they said they never thought about the drowned houses and streets. When I spoke to some people sitting in the café overlooking the lake, I was surprised to find they still feel angry about what happened. They used to live in Vinnthorpe and were moved to other places in the area, among them thirty children who are now middle-aged, but they still miss the village. They say that nobody asked them what they wanted – they were told one day that everything was decided. It is a shame that these people lost their homes and I hope something similar never happens again in the future. I would miss the watersports if they weren't there, however, and I must say that I hadn't ever thought about what was under the water until last week.

Look at Questions 21–25 below.

It is important to understand the questions before reading the text in more detail. This exercise will help you to think about the questions.

Underline the best word or phrase to complete each sentence.

1 Look at Question 21. This is always a general question.

   This question asks about the writer's *purpose / hobbies / friends*.

2 Look at Question 22. This is usually a general question.

   This question asks about *who wrote the text / what the text tells you / when the text was written*.

3 Look at Question 23. This question always asks about detail or opinion.

   This question asks about *attitudes towards / information about / ideas about* Lake Vinney.

4 Look at Question 24. This question always asks about detail or opinion.

   This question asks about the writer's *plans / attitude / discovery*.

5 Look at Question 25. This is always a general question.

   This question asks about a way of *persuading people to visit / warning people of a danger / telling people about changes*.

▶▶ Exam tip!

If you are not sure of the answer to one question, do the others and come back to it at the end. It may be easier then.

 Finish the exam task.

   Read the text carefully and choose the correct answer for each question. Mark your answers on your answer sheet.

▶ Key strategy

Complete the following:

Read the text quickly to get a general idea. Read the questions carefully, then go back to the text and look for ....

(If you don't remember, look at page 18.)

---

21 What is the writer trying to do?

   A describe what people think about the drowned village

   B persuade people to take up watersports on Lake Vinney

   C discuss what might happen to Lake Vinney in the future

   D explain why people like living by Lake Vinney

22 What can a reader find out from the text?

   A how electricity is produced

   B how many people used to live in Vinnthorpe

   C who decided to drown the village

   D why some people feel annoyed

23 What do we find out about Lake Vinney?

   A It attracts tourists from abroad.

   B There are lots of houses on the banks.

   C More people are visiting it every year.

   D Mainly local people do watersports there.

24 What does the writer think about Vinnthorpe?

   A He agrees with Pat Smithers.

   B He feels sorry for the people who lived there.

   C He thinks it should now be forgotten.

   D He has always felt guilty about water-skiing there.

25 Which of these is an advert for Lake Vinney?

A
> Come to Lake Vinney and water-ski or sail. No ugly car parks, shops or cafés around the lake to spoil the views.

B
> Come to Vinnthorpe and stay in a hotel in the village. Enjoy the walks around the lake in complete peace and quiet.

C
> Lake Vinney is perfect for all kinds of watersports. Wonderful café by the side of the lake and plenty of car parking space.

D
> Enjoy water-skiing on Lake Vinney but leave time to visit the old village beside the lake – nothing has changed there for 30 years.

▷▷ Extra language practice

1▶ Grammar: reported speech

In the text, the writer reports what people said:
... they said they never thought about the drowned houses ...

The people actually said:
'We never think about the drowned houses.'

Look at the sentences below and write what the speakers actually said in your notebook.

Example:
He said he didn't want any coffee.   *'I don't want any coffee.'*

1 They said the book was in the post.
2 She explained she didn't usually work there.
3 She told us she was going home.
4 You said you expected to arrive before lunch.
5 We said we would help with the housework at the weekend.

2▶ Vocabulary: fuels

a) Match the words in the box to the pictures below. The first one is done for you.

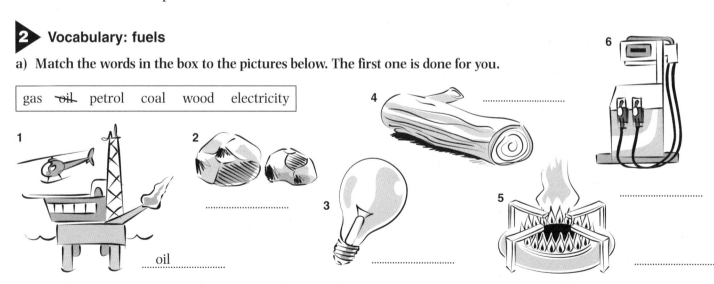

gas ~~oil~~ petrol coal wood electricity

1 .... oil
2 ....
3 ....
4 ....
5 ....
6 ....

b) Which fuels do you use in your home?

1 We cook with ....
2 We heat our home with ....
3 We run our car on ....
4 Trains can run on ....
5 Electricity can be made by burning ....
6 When people go camping, they make fires with ....

Part 5

In Part 5 there is a text with numbered spaces.
You need to choose the correct word to fill each space.

1 Read the instructions to the exam task on the opposite page.

1 What do you have to read?
2 What do you have to choose?
3 Where do you put your answers?

2 Look at the text heading and make guesses about the text.
Which of the following people do you think the text might be about?

- a man who lives in an airport
- a man who works in an airport
- a man who likes visiting airports
- a man who owns an airport
- a man who builds airports
- a man who designs airports

3 Read the text quickly and check your guesses.
Did you guess correctly? Don't worry about the spaces for now.

4 Look at the example (0).
Read the first sentence of the text carefully. What is the answer to Question (0)?

5 Look at Questions 26–35.
For each question, read the whole of the sentence which contains the space.
Choose your answers for the ones you are certain about. Write the words in the
spaces – they may help you to understand the text.

▶▶ Exam tip!

Remember that the word you need must fit the grammar of the space as well as
the meaning.

6 Finish the exam task.
Now go back and guess the other answers. When you have done all the
questions, mark your answers on your answer sheet. Check that you are putting
them in the right place.

Key strategy

Complete the following:

Read the .... before you start thinking about the spaces.
Then, choose the best answer for each space. Leave the ones you are not sure about
until the end – the answers may become clearer then.

(If you don't remember, look at page 20.)

Part 5

Questions 26–35

- Read the text below and choose the correct word for each space.
- For each question, mark the letter next to the correct word – **A**, **B**, **C** or **D** – **on your answer sheet**.

Example answer:

Part 5				
0	**A** ■	**B** ☐	**C** ☐	**D** ☐

The airport man

Yesterday Ahmed **(0)** .... his home for the first time in eleven years. But his home is a very unusual one – he has **(26)** .... the last eleven years living in an international airport. Ahmed had no family in his own country so eleven years ago he set off to search **(27)** .... his sister who lived in Scotland. He hadn't heard from her for **(28)** .... but he had an old address. He never **(29)** .... Scotland, however, because while he was **(30)** .... for a connecting flight, all his documents **(31)** .... stolen and he had to ask for new ones. **(32)** .... he had nowhere to go, he stayed in the airport. After a **(33)** .... weeks he was still there. He became **(34)** .... as 'Sir George' and all the airport staff liked him. Eleven years **(35)** .... his documents arrived and he was free to go. But he no longer wanted to!

0	**A** left	**B** went	**C** removed	**D** departed
26	**A** taken	**B** passed	**C** spent	**D** used
27	**A** to	**B** for	**C** from	**D** at
28	**A** years	**B** times	**C** long	**D** ever
29	**A** got	**B** arrived	**C** travelled	**D** reached
30	**A** waiting	**B** thinking	**C** booking	**D** sitting
31	**A** had	**B** were	**C** are	**D** have
32	**A** Although	**B** Even	**C** As	**D** If
33	**A** several	**B** many	**C** lot	**D** few
34	**A** called	**B** known	**C** told	**D** said
35	**A** following	**B** since	**C** later	**D** next

Extra language practice

 Vocabulary: at the airport

a) Choose three people and three places from the following list. Write a sentence explaining what each one is. Use the language in the box below to help you.

- air hostess
- baggage hall
- check-in desk
- customs officer
- departure lounge
- duty-free shop
- immigration officer
- information desk
- passenger
- pilot
- snack bar

Useful language

This is someone who ...
This is the person who ...
This is the place where ...

Example:
This is someone who flies an aeroplane. *(pilot)*

b) Work with a partner. Read aloud what you have written. Your partner will guess which person or place you are describing.

c) Now imagine that you are at the airport and that you are going to fly somewhere. With your partner, think of the order in which you might go to the places in the list.

Example:
When you arrive at the airport, you go to the check-in desk, then you ...

 Speaking: an interview

Work with a partner.

Student A: You are a journalist. You have to interview Ahmed and ask him about his life in the airport. Think about the kinds of questions you are going to ask. Look in the box below for suggestions.

Where How	did you	sleep? eat? wash your clothes? get enough food?

Student B: You are Ahmed. Look at the box above and try to think of some answers.

Grammar: prepositions

In Part 5 you often need to know which preposition (if any) follows a certain verb. For example, in the example (0), we know that B and D are not the answer because it's wrong to say *went his home* or *departed his home*, we must say *went away from*, or *departed from*.

Look at the following sentences. Each verb is followed by a space. Decide whether you need to put a preposition in each space. If you do need a preposition, decide which one. The first one is done for you.

1 We lived *.in.* Rome when I was young.
2 A thief stole .... my purse when I was on the train.
3 What time does the ferry arrive .... the island?
4 Please put .... all the books when you have finished.
5 We didn't reach .... London until late at night.
6 I'm staying .... my cousins while my parents are away.
7 Nobody can enter .... the theatre until the actors are ready.
8 Take the dirty cups .... the tray and put them in the cupboard.
9 Please can you pass .... me the sugar?
10 Did you get .... home very late last night?

Writing

Part 1

In Part 1 you read some sentences and then you rewrite them using a different grammar pattern.

 Read the instructions to the exam task below.

1 How many sentences are there?
2 What are the sentences about?
3 What do you have to do?
4 Where do you write your answers?
5 How much do you write there?
6 Where can you do your rough work?

 Look at the example.

1 Read the first sentence. What information does it give you about the school?
2 Now read the second sentence. Does it give you the same information as the first sentence?

 Look at Question 1.

1 Read the first sentence. What information does it give you about the school?
2 Now read the beginning of the second sentence. How does it begin?
3 How can you complete it? Write your answer. (If you are not sure about your answer, write it on the exam paper first and read it carefully before you copy it.)
4 Check your answer. Does your sentence give the same information as the first sentence? Is the grammar correct?

▶▶ Exam tip!

Make sure that your sentence includes all the information from the sentence you are given.

Part 1

Questions 1–5

- Here are some sentences about a language school.
- For each question, finish the second sentence so that it means the same as the first.
- The second sentence is started for you. **Write only the missing words on your answer sheet.**
- You may use this page for any rough work.

Example: The school is near the station.

This school is ..*not far from the station.*..

1 The school opened five years ago.

The school has been here..

4 ► Language focus 1: grammar patterns

In Part 1, the same grammar patterns are often tested. It is a good idea to study these patterns so that you can recognise them.

a) Look at the example on page 69 again.

The pattern here is: *X is near Y. = X is not far from Y.*

What is the pattern in Question 1? Write it here:
X opened ... years ago. = Y has been open ....

b) Read the ten sentences below. There are five pairs which have the same meanings. Can you find them?

Example: 1, 7

1   The waiter said I should try the fish soup.
2   It has fifty tables.
3   The restaurant is not far from the river.
4   The meals cost more in the evening.
5   There are fifty tables.

6   My girlfriend said 'I really enjoyed my meal'.
7   The waiter advised me to try the fish soup.
8   My girlfriend told me she had really enjoyed her meal.
9   The restaurant is near the river.
10 In the evenings the meals are more expensive.

5 ► Finish the exam task.

Write the answers to Questions 2–5 on your answer sheet. Remember you can write them on the exam paper first if you wish and then copy them.

► Key strategy

Complete the following:

Think carefully about the meaning of the first sentence. When you complete the second sentence, make sure it means .... as the first one.

(If you don't remember, look at page 24.)

2   Each class has twelve students.

There ....

3   The school advised me to book early.

The school said I ....

4   The courses cost more in August.

In August the courses are ....

5   My friend said 'I enjoyed studying there'.

My friend told me she ....

6 ▶ Language focus 2: checking mistakes

Read these pairs of sentences. They should mean the same thing. The second sentence in each pair is wrong. Can you correct it?

Example:
He is called Robert.
His name is ~~called~~ Robert.

1 My flat isn't as big as yours.
   My flat is smaller as yours.

2 My brother is a member of the tennis club.
   My brother is belong to the tennis club.

3 My sister suggested I should go swimming with her.
   'Why not you come swimming with me?' suggested my sister.

4 You can't get a table unless you book.
   You can get a table if you don't book.

5 I like modern shops better than old ones.
   I prefer modern shops from old ones.

7 ▶ Check your answers to the exam task.

Read your answers and correct any mistakes. Then exchange your answers with another student and correct any mistakes you find.

▷▷ Extra language practice

1 ▶ Speaking about your school

Spend two minutes thinking about the school where you study. Imagine you have to give a talk about it to some visitors. What would you say? Use the expressions in the box to help you.

> **Useful language**
>
> The students are usually …
> The school has …
> Most of the students enjoy …
> Nobody likes …
> The best classes …
> We have lots of …
> There aren't any …

When you are ready, work with a partner. Talk about your school for one minute. Then listen to what your partner has to say. Did you talk about the same things? Do you agree with each other's opinions?

2 ▶ Grammar: verbs + *to* or *should*

> Look at Question 3 on page 70. This tests the grammar which follows the verbs *say* and *advise*. There are some other important verbs which you will meet in the exam and which follow similar rules. You need to learn how they work.

Complete the sentences using *should* or *to*. The first one is done for you.

1 Before the race, the teacher advised the students *to* do some exercises.

2 Because the weather was bad, Sue said the children ……………… stay indoors.

3 The manager asked her assistant ……………… post a letter for her.

4 The hotel owner invited the guests ……………… use the swimming pool.

5 In order to save their money, John suggested his friends ……………… take the bus.

6 The angry traveller insisted that the bus driver ……………… return his money.

7 The shop assistant persuaded my mother ……………… try a different style of coat.

Part 2

> In Part 2 you are given a form.
> You have to fill in information about yourself on the form.

 1 Read the instructions to the exam task on the opposite page.

1 What do you want to do?
2 Who has sent you a form?
3 What kind of form is it?
4 Where do you write your answers?
5 Where can you do your rough work?

2 Language focus: geography

> In the exam you often need to understand the language used to explain where a place is.

Look at the map of Britain. Then complete the sentences below using phrases from the box. The first one is done for you.

---

on the south coast of   in the west of
in the north-west of   in the north of
just off the south coast of   near the east coast of
~~in the south-east of~~

---

1 London is .in.the.south-east.of. England.
2 Cardiff is .... Wales.
3 Edinburgh is .... Scotland.
4 Bath is .... England.
5 Loch Ness is .... Scotland.
6 The Isle of Wight is .... England.
7 Snowdonia National Park is .... Wales.

3 Look at the exam task on the opposite page and decide what information is needed.

1 Which questions can you answer using a number or a letter?
2 Where will you need to write a date?
3 Will you need to sign your name or spell it out in full?
4 Think about possible different answers to Questions 11–15.

4 Write your answers.
Now fill in your own answers for Questions 6–15. For Questions 6–10 you must give true answers. For Questions 11–15 you can use your imagination if you want. Write your answers on your answer sheet. Remember you can write them on the exam paper first if you wish and then copy them.

 Exam tip!

If you are not sure how to spell a word, give a different answer which you can spell correctly.

5 Check your answers.
Use these questions to help you check your answers to the exam task on the opposite page.

Question 6: Did you put all your names?
Question 7: Did you remember to put your country? Did you use a capital letter at the beginning?
Question 8: Did you put a number?
Question 9: Did you put female / F or male / M?
Question 10: Did you spell this correctly?
Question 11: Did you write a way of travelling?
Question 12: Did you give a geographical region or the name of a place?
Question 13: Did you give a length of time?
Question 14: Did you give a future date, including the day, month and year?
Question 15: Did you write the names of two meals and spell them correctly?

> **Exam strategy**
> *Complete the following:*
> **Make sure you give sensible answers and that your .... is correct.**
> *(If you don't remember, look at page 27.)*

Part 2

Questions 6–15

- You want to stay with a family in Britain.
- An agency sends you a questionnaire to complete.
- Look at the questionnaire and answer each question.
- **Write your answers on your answer sheet.**
- You may use this page for any rough work.

Castle Square
Southside   ST4 4RT
UK

Family stay questionnaire

Full name: (**6**) ....

Home address (including country): (**7**) ....

....

Age: (**8**) ....

Sex: (**9**) ....

Nationality: (**10**) ....

How will you travel to Britain? (**11**) ....

Which part of Britain do you want to visit? (**12**) ....

How long will you stay in Britain? (**13**) ....

When will you arrive (day / month / year)? (**14**) ....

Which two meals do you want to eat with the family? (**15**) ....

....

Extra language practice

 Vocabulary: food

In the exam you often have to read, write or speak about food.

Here are some of the names of food you may meet in the exam. Use a dictionary to check any that you don't know. Write the words under the correct headings in your notebook.

bacon	banana	~~bean~~	beef	cabbage	cake	carrot	cauliflower	cod
grape	ham	ice cream	lamb	lemon	mushroom	pastry	pea	pie
plaice	pork	potato	poultry	rice	spinach	strawberry	tart	tomato

vegetables	fruit	meat	fish	dessert
bean				

 Speaking: visiting Britain

Look at the information on the right about visiting different places in Britain. Think about:

- the city you would like to visit
- what you would like to do there
- what you would like to buy
- what other parts of Britain you would like to visit
- what you could see there

Work with a partner. Ask your partner which city he / she would like to visit and why.

Example:
'I'd like to visit Edinburgh because I love castles.'

Do you both want to visit the same place and do the same things?

London:
❏ explore the capital of England and the home of English kings and queens
❏ visit museums, cathedrals and palaces
❏ go shopping on world-famous Oxford Street or at any of the big department stores

Edinburgh:
❏ visit Edinburgh Castle
❏ travel to Loch Ness, home of the Loch Ness monster
❏ enjoy trips into the beautiful Scottish countryside

Cardiff:
❏ visit the old city centre
❏ go to a rugby match
❏ explore the beautiful Welsh coast

3 ▶ Writing a postcard

Imagine you are on a short holiday in Britain. You are writing a postcard to your classmates. Write about where you are. Say what you have seen and where you want to go next.
Exchange cards with another student. Check each other's writing. Help each other to correct any mistakes.

> In Part 3 you have to write a letter.

 Read the instructions to the exam task below.

1 Who are you going to write to?
2 Why are you writing?
3 The question tells you to write about three things. What are they?
4 How many words must you write?
5 Where must you write your answer?
6 How will the answer begin?

 Plan your answer.

Before starting your letter, it is important to make a plan. This will help you to concentrate on your English when you begin to write. Remember, you have to write about three things.

Look at your answer to question 3 in Exercise 1. Make notes of your ideas for the three parts of the question.

> ▶▶ **Exam tip!**

In the exam you can make a plan on the exam paper before you start writing on your answer sheet.

Part 3

Question 16

- You have just moved to a new house or flat.
- You are writing a letter to an English-speaking friend to tell them about it.
- Describe your new house or flat, say what you like best about it and say how it is different from where you lived before.
- **Finish the letter on your answer sheet, using about 100 words.**

Dear . . . . . ,

I moved last week and I'm writing to tell you where I'm living now. ....

....

> You must write your answers on
> the separate answer sheet.

3 Language focus 1: describing houses and flats

In your letter you will have to describe your new accommodation. Use the words in the boxes to label the pictures. Use a dictionary to help you.

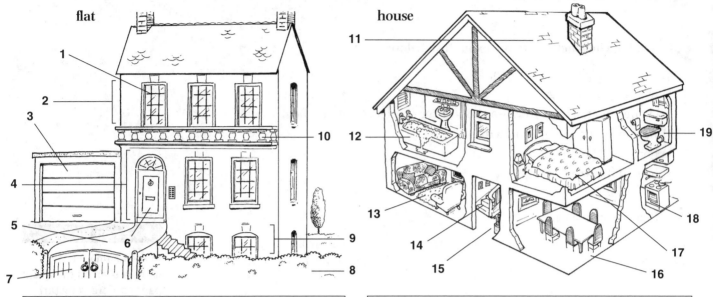

flat

house

| basement | first floor | ground floor | front door |
| path | window | gate | hedge | garage | balcony |

| kitchen | dining room | sitting room | bedroom |
| bathroom | toilet | hall | roof | stairs |

room

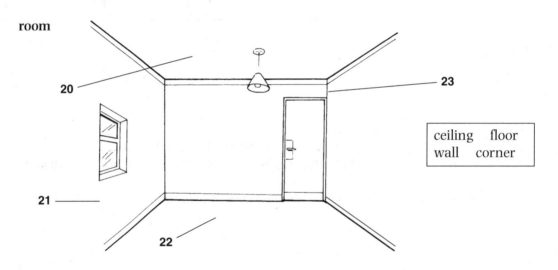

| ceiling | floor |
| wall | corner |

▶▶ **Exam tip!**

The question always has three parts. Make sure you write about all three of them.

4 Write your letter.

Look at the notes you made in Exercise 2 and think about the vocabulary you studied in Exercise 3. Now write your own letter on your answer sheet.

> **Key strategy**
>
> *Complete the following:*
>
> **Read the instructions and make sure you understand what you have to write about and why. .... what you will say, then write your answer. Finally, check your answer for any ....**
>
> *(If you don't remember, look at page 30.)*

Language focus 2: correcting mistakes

Read the following sentences. Each one has two mistakes. Correct them and say what sort of mistakes they are – punctuation, spelling, verb.

1 Last week I saw a computer in the shoping centre that I really want have.
2 I've saved enough money by working in my cousins garage on saturdays.
3 When I starts university in the autum, I'll need one.
4 But if I am buying the computer, I wont be able to go on holiday.
5 So I must to decide which will make me happyest!

 Check your letter for mistakes.
    Read your letter again and correct any mistakes. Exchange your letter with another student and correct any mistakes you find.

▷▷ **Extra language practice**

 Speaking about where you live

a) Think about the town where you live. Think about:

- things to do   • things to see   • activities for young people   • parks
- museums   • traffic   • transport

In your notebook, write down the two things you like best about your town and the two things you like least about your town.

b) Work with a partner. Discuss the things you wrote. Do you agree? What about?

2 **Grammar: comparisons**

> In the exam you will often be asked to compare two or more things. Make sure you know the structures you need to do this.

Look at these sentences.

My new flat is	quieter than nicer than bigger than noisier more comfortable than not as expensive as	the old one.	*quiet + er* *nice + r* *big + g + er* *noisy − y + ier* *more + comfortable* *not as + expensive + as*

Rewrite these sentences in your notebook using the word in brackets.

Example:
I / my father (tall)
I am taller than my father.   OR   *I am not as tall as my father.*

1 My writing / my friend's writing (tidy)
2 History / science (interesting)
3 Scotland / Italy (wet)
4 I / my brother, cousin, etc. (lazy)
5 Motor racing / water-skiing (dangerous)
6 The sun / the moon (bright)
7 The north of Australia / the south of Australia (hot)
8 Speaking English / writing English (easy)

Part 1

> In Part 1 you hear seven different recordings. Sometimes there is one speaker and sometimes there are two.
>
> You listen and choose the correct picture by choosing A, B, C or D.

1 ▶ 📼 Read and listen to the instructions to the exam task on the opposite page.

1 How many questions are there?
2 How many pictures are there for each question?
3 How many times will you hear each recording?
4 What do you have to do?

> At the end of the exam you are given 12 minutes to transfer all your listening answers to the answer sheet. Make sure you copy carefully.

2 ▶ 📼 Look at the example on the opposite page and listen to the recording.

1 What is the question?
2 What is the answer?
3 How do you know?

▶▶ Exam tip!

Remember you will hear each recording twice before you hear the next one so, if you can't find the answer the first time you hear, you have another chance immediately.

3 ▶ Language focus: weather

> In Part 1 there is often a question about the weather.

a) Look at the exam task. Which question is about the weather?

b) Match the following sentences to the pictures on the right. Some sentences can be used with more than one picture.

- It's sunny.
- It's windy.
- It's foggy.
- It's cloudy.
- It's misty.
- It's icy.
- It's frosty.
- It's snowing.
- It's raining.
- It's freezing.
- It's damp.
- It's wet.
- It's hot.

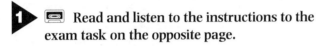

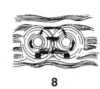

1　　　　2　　　　3

4　　　5　　　6

7　　　8　　　9

4 ▶ 📼 Look at Question 1.

1 What information must you listen for?
2 Look at the four pictures. What are the names of the places in pictures A, B, C and D?
3 Listen to the recording for Question 1. Which of the places did you hear?
4 Listen again and mark your answer.
5 Why is A wrong?
6 Why is B wrong?
7 Why is D wrong?
8 Why is C the correct answer? What does the woman say?

5 ▶ 📼 Look at Question 2.

1 What information must you listen for?
2 Look at the four pictures. What words do you think you might hear?
3 Listen to the recording for Question 2 and mark your answer.
4 Listen again and check your answer.

6 ▶ Finish the exam task.
　Now do Questions 3–7 in the same way.

> ### ▶ Key strategy
>
> *Complete the following:*
>
> **Use the .... to help you. You can guess a lot about what you are going to hear by looking at them.**
>
> *(If you don't remember, look at page 32.)*

Part 1

Questions 1–7

- There are seven questions in this Part.
- For each question there are four pictures and a short recording.
- You will hear each recording twice.
- For each question, look at the pictures and listen to the recording.
- Choose the correct picture and put a tick (✓) in the box below it.

Example: Which train will the woman catch?

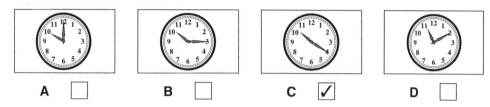

A ☐   B ☐   C ✓   D ☐

1 Where will they meet?

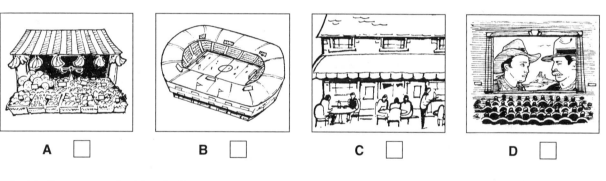

A ☐   B ☐   C ☐   D ☐

2 What is the woman looking for?

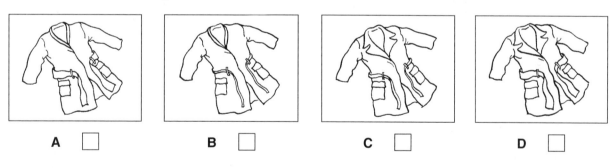

A ☐   B ☐   C ☐   D ☐

3 Which photograph are they looking at?

A ☐   B ☐   C ☐   D ☐

[Turn over

4 Which post is for the woman?

A ☐   B ☐   C ☐   D ☐

5 Who is coming to stay with the girl?

A ☐   B ☐   C ☐   D ☐

6 What was the weather like on Tom's holiday?

A ☐   B ☐   C ☐   D ☐

7 Where is the desk now?

A ☐   B ☐   C ☐   D ☐

▷▷ **Extra language practice**

Vocabulary: clothes

In Part 1 you may hear people describing clothes.

Here are some words that you may meet in the exam. Decide which of the words in the box belong with the different clothes. (Some of them can go in all the columns!) The first one is done for you.

| b̶e̶l̶t̶ V-neck silk knee-length pockets |
| collar short sleeves buttons zip round neck |
| leather high heels sleeveless wool cotton |

skirt	coat	jacket	dress	shirt	boots
belt	belt	belt	belt		

> In Part 2 you hear one person speaking. They may be talking to a group of people or on the radio.
>
> You listen and answer the questions by choosing A, B, C or D.

1 Read and listen to the instructions to the exam task below.

1 How many questions are there?
2 Who will you hear?
3 Who is he talking to?
4 What is he talking about?
5 What do you have to do?
6 How many times will you hear the recording?

 Pronunciation focus: short verb forms

> When people speak they usually use short verb forms. They do this in the exam recordings but on the exam paper the verbs are usually written in full.

Look at these verbs you will hear in the recording. Write the short forms of the verbs.

Example:
I would just like to check. *I'd just like to check.*

1 We have lots to do.
2 Breakfast is available.
3 We will be back on the road.
4 I have found a pleasant way to save time.
5 That was not the only exciting discovery.
6 Do not miss the walls and floor.
7 They are made of local stone.
8 You are not too tired.

Now practise saying the sentences using the short forms.

Part 2

Questions 8–13

- Look at the questions for this Part.
- You will hear a tour guide talking to a group of tourists about plans for the next day.
- Put a tick (✓) in the correct box for each question.

3 Look at the exam task on the next page and make guesses.

Which of the following do you think the guide will talk about? Use the questions to put them in the right order.

- visit a museum
- look around an old building
- see jewellery being made
- leave their hotel
- have an evening meal
- go to a concert in an old building
- see people in traditional clothes
- visit a gallery
- have lunch

 Exam tip!

You must choose the answer which really gives the information asked for in the question, so read the question very carefully.

4 Listen to the recording.
The questions always follow the same order as what you hear on the recording.

1 Look at Question 8. Listen to what the tour guide says about the coach leaving and tick the correct answer. Be careful – she says all the other times but only one of them is about the coach leaving!

2 Look at Question 9. Listen to what they will see in the gallery. Tick the correct answer.

3 Now do Questions 10–13 in the same way. Don't worry if you don't get all the answers the first time. You will hear the recording twice.

5 📼 Listen to the recording again.
   Check the answers you have marked and try to do any you missed the first time.
If you still don't know, guess! Do not leave any questions unanswered.

Key strategy

Complete the following:

Use the questions to help you understand the recording. The second time you listen, ... your answers and answer those you missed the first time.

(If you don't remember, look at page 36.)

8 What time does the coach leave in the morning?

    A ☐ 8.15

    B ☐ 8.25

    C ☐ 8.30

    D ☐ 9.45

9 What will they see in the gallery?

    A ☐ paintings

    B ☐ photographs

    C ☐ sculptures

    D ☐ glass

10 Where will they eat lunch?

    A ☐ on the coach

    B ☐ outside the gallery

    C ☐ in a park

    D ☐ beside the lake

11 What will they visit in the afternoon?

    A ☐ a castle

    B ☐ a house

    C ☐ a church

    D ☐ a temple

12 What can they see inside the building?

    A ☐ painted walls

    B ☐ wooden floors

    C ☐ golden doors

    D ☐ silver furniture

13 Where does the tour guide suggest eating in the evening?

    A ☐ at the hotel

    B ☐ in the market place

    C ☐ by the river

    D ☐ on a boat

▷▷ Extra language practice

Speaking: planning a day out

Work with a partner. Plan a day out on a coach for your class. Decide:

- what time you will leave and come back
- where you will go (the seaside, a park, a sports centre, a museum, a shopping centre?)
- where you will eat (a fast food bar, an expensive restaurant, a picnic area?).

Use the language in the box to help you.

Useful language

Why don't we ...   Let's ...   We could ...
After going to ... we can ...

---

2 ▷ **Grammar: possessives**

Look at these phrases from the recording.

- *the **area's** most interesting gallery*
- ***people's** everyday life*
- *the **artists'** skills*

a) **Why is the apostrophe (') in a different place in *area's* and *artists'*? Is *people* a singular word or plural word? What is unusual about *people's*?**

b) **Rewrite the sentences in your notebook with the apostrophe in the correct place.**

   Example:
   When he got angry, you could hear my fathers voice in the next street.

   When he got angry, you could hear my father's voice in the next street.

1 I have two boys and two girls – the boys school is near our house but the girls school is three kilometres away.

2 I looked through all the womens' clothes in the shop but there was nothing suitable.

3 I tried not to laugh when I saw Janes new hairstyle.

4 Her friends parents all agreed that the party should finish at eleven.

5 The childrens grandfather took them to the seaside.

---

3 ▷ **Vocabulary: museum objects**

Here are some things which you might see in a museum. Match the words in the box with the pictures below.

---

carpet   painting   weapons   jewellery   glass
antique furniture   pottery   ~~sculpture~~   toy
some old coins

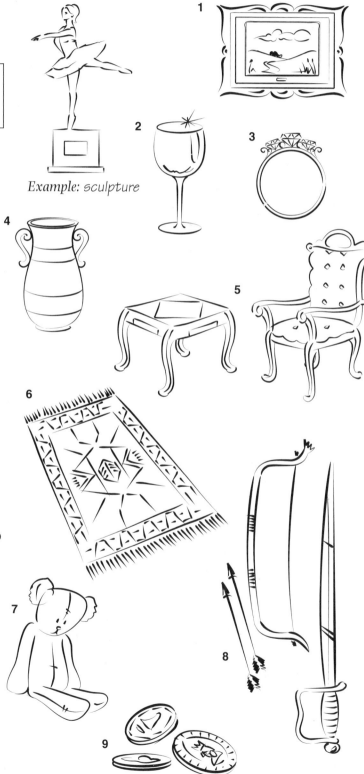

Example: sculpture

Part 3

> In Part 3 you hear one person speaking. He or she gives information to a group of people or on the radio.
> You read some notes and fill in missing information.

1 📼 Read and listen to the instructions to the exam task on the opposite page.

1 How many questions are there?
2 Who will you hear? What will she talk about?
3 What do you have to do?
4 How many times will you hear the recording?

2 Language focus: writing dates and numbers

In Part 3, it is important to be able to write dates and numbers correctly.

a) Look at the exam task. Where must you write a date or number?

b) Write the following dates correctly.

Example:
teusday 9th juli 2015
Tuesday 9th July 2015

1 febuary 21th 2002
2 wensday 2 marsh 2005
3 septembre 4st 2009
4 thrusday aprille 19th 2020

c) Write the following numbers in figures.

Example:
a hundred and five
105

1 one thousand, three hundred and ten
2 fifteen hundred
3 three hundred thousand
4 thirty thousand, five hundred

d) Listen to your teacher read some dates and numbers and write them down. Be careful with your spelling and punctuation.

3 Look at the task and guess what kinds of words are missing.

1 Look at Question 14. What kind of word can go in this space? How do you know?
2 Look at Question 15. What kind of word can go in this space? How do you know?
3 Look at Question 16. What kind of word can go in this space? How do you know?
4 Look at Question 17. What kind of information do you need here? How do you know?
5 Look at Question 18. What kind of information do you need here? How do you know?
6 Look at Question 19. What sort of word can go here? How do you know?

4 📼 Listen to the recording.
Try to answer as many questions as you can. If you miss a gap, don't worry. You can fill it in the second time you listen.

▶▶ **Exam tip!**

You usually need to write one or two words and never more than three.

5 📼 Listen to the recording again.
Check the answers you wrote the first time. Fill in any answers you missed.

6 Check your answers.

1 How many words did you write in each space?
2 Is the meaning correct?
3 Is the grammar correct?
4 Is the spelling correct?

> **Key Strategy**
> *Complete the following:*
> **Before you listen, look at the spaces and decide what .... you need. Then listen for that information.**
> *(If you don't remember, look at page 39.)*

Part 3

Questions 14–19

- Look at the notes about a competition.
- Some information is missing.
- You will hear a woman talking on the radio about the competition.
- For each question, fill in the missing information in the numbered space.

This month's competition

Prize: a computer + a (**14**) .... printer

Write a story

    length: less than (**15**) .... words

    subject: a short (**16**) .... story which takes place in

    (**17**) ....

Write your name, address, telephone number and (**18**) ....

at the end.

Story must arrive on or before (**19**) ....

Extra language practice

1 Speaking: a competition

Work with a partner.

Look at the following ideas for a school competition. Which do you think is the most interesting?

- a sports quiz
- a race
- a spelling quiz
- a drawing competition

You and your partner are organising one of these competitions for your class.

- Which competition are you going to organise?
- What will the students have to do?
- What are the rules?
- What will the prize be?

> **Useful language**
>
> Everyone must ...
> No one can ...
> The first prize will be ...

2 Vocabulary: adjectives

Look at what the woman says on the recording.

- *'our **super** new competition'*
- *'**short** story'*
- *'the rules are very **simple**'*
- *'they can be **strange** and **wonderful**'*

The **bold** words are all adjectives and they all describe something.

Write two sentences about each of the pictures below using the adjectives in the box. Use these sentence patterns to help you.

- The woman looks ...
- The woman is ...
- What a ... woman!

strange	lucky
friendly	useful
expensive	useless
fast	wonderful
interesting	frightening
comfortable	boring
old	beautiful
amazing	dull
out of date	

3 Vocabulary: computer words

Use the words in the box to label the pictures (1–6) and complete the sentences (7–11).

screen	CD	printer	keyboard	disk	speakers
mouse	e-mail	software	Internet	fax	

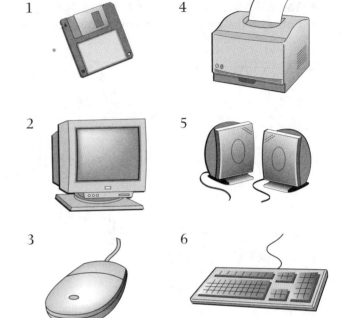

1

4

2

5

3

6

7 You can get information on almost any subject on the ....

8 You need .... in order to run a particular computer program.

9 Music and information can be found on a ....

10 You can send a document from your computer or by using a special .... machine.

11 Instead of writing a letter to someone, you can send an .... on your computer.

Part 4

> In Part 4 you hear two people having a conversation and you read some statements.
>
> You must decide whether each statement is correct or incorrect.

1 Read and listen to the instructions to the exam task below.

1 How many statements are there?
2 How many people will you hear?
3 What is the man's name?
4 What is the woman's name?
5 How do they know each other?
6 What do you have to do?
7 How many times will you hear the recording?

> Remember, at the end of the exam you are given twelve minutes to transfer all your listening answers to the answer sheet. Make sure you copy carefully.

2 Language focus: agreeing and disagreeing

> In Part 4 you often need to understand when people are agreeing and disagreeing with each other.

a) Look at the phrases. Write *A* next to the ones which you use to agree, and *D* next to the ones which you use to disagree. The first one is done for you.

a) I don't think so.   *D*
b) That's not right.
c) I quite agree.
d) Exactly.
e) I just don't accept that.
f) I don't agree.
g) That's where you're wrong.
h) That's right.

b) Read the conversation below between two women, Suzie and Carol. For each space, decide whether the speaker is agreeing or disagreeing and choose one of the phrases to fill it.

Suzie: I worry about teenagers today. They spend all their free time sitting in front of computers. It's a real waste of time.

Carol: (1) .... because a lot of the time they're actually learning something. And it's the best way nowadays to find out information.

Suzie: (2) ....What's wrong with books? Anyway, I don't think they work hard enough. Not as hard as we did at school.

Carol: (3) .... I think they work harder than we did. I'm jealous of my daughter – they have so many opportunities – all the different subjects they can study.

Suzie: (4) .... There are so many interesting ones to choose from. And so many of them travel these days. My daughter's been to more foreign countries than me. I think it's better to wait till you're a bit older and you understand more about life.

Carol: (5) .... It's all part of learning and it's especially useful if you're learning foreign languages.

Suzie: (6) .... It does help if you get a chance to practise. Maybe that's why I was never good at languages. I was good at sport though. Teenagers don't seem interested any more.

Carol: (7) .... They just enjoy different sports from us. But I don't think they're as fit as we were because we had to walk everywhere. We weren't driven about by car.

Suzie: (8) .... I was much fitter before I had a car.

Part 4

Questions 20–25

- Look at the six statements for this Part.
- You will hear a conversation between a man, Marcus, and a woman, Cora, who work in the same office.
- Decide if you think each statement is correct or incorrect.
- If you think it is correct, put a tick (✔) in the box under **A** for **YES**. If you think it is not correct, put a tick (✔) in the box under **B** for **NO**.

Exam tip!

When a question is about agreeing or disagreeing, you need to listen carefully to what both speakers say on that subject.

3 Look at the exam task below and make guesses. Underline six words or phrases which tell you what Marcus and Cora's conversation will be about. Compare your list of words with another student.

4 Listen to the recording and answer the questions.
If you miss one, don't worry. You can listen for the answer when you hear the recording again.

5 Listen to the recording again and check your answers.
Try to fill in any answers you missed the first time. If you still don't know, guess! Do not leave any questions unanswered.

Key strategy
Complete the following:

Try to read the statements as you listen but the words you hear may not be exactly the same as the words in the ....

(If you don't remember, look at page 42.)

		A YES	B NO
20	Marcus is often late for work.	☐	☐
21	Cora disagrees with Marcus about the cause of traffic jams.	☐	☐
22	Marcus agrees that cycling to work would be good for him.	☐	☐
23	Marcus believes employers should provide buses.	☐	☐
24	Marcus agrees to try coming to work by bus tomorrow.	☐	☐
25	Cora suggests that Marcus is lazy.	☐	☐

▷▷ Extra language practice

 Vocabulary: traffic

In the exam you often meet or need to use words about traffic problems.

Complete the following sentences with a word or phrase from the box. The first one is done for you.

motorways   bus stop   car park   ~~pollution~~
speed limit   roundabout   parking space   traffic
pedestrian   crossroads   traffic jam   traffic lights

1 The ..*pollution*.. in some city centres is so bad it is difficult to breathe.

2 Someone took my .... in the .... today, so I had to park in the street.

3 The car didn't stop at the .... even though they were red and nearly knocked over a .... who was trying to cross the road.

4 The .... on .... is 90 kph which is higher than on ordinary roads.

5 Follow the road past the park, go round the ...., turn left at the .... and my house is on the left.

6 I never drive through the city centre because there's always a .... by the bus station.

7 There was so much .... the bus was delayed and I waited at the .... for half an hour.

2 ▶ Speaking: traffic

a) Here are some ideas for reducing traffic in big cities. Tick the sentences that you agree with.

- The government should encourage people to use buses and trains.
- One idea is to make petrol more expensive.
- Another idea is to make bus tickets cheaper.
- Each family should have only one car.

b) Now work with a partner.
Discuss the best ways of reducing traffic in the town where you live or in the capital city of your country.

Useful language

Phrases:
The government could ...
It would help if we ...
One idea is to ...
Another idea is to ...

Verbs:
stop   prevent   persuade   encourage   forbid

3 ▶ Grammar: *get*

Get is a very common word in English and has lots of different meanings. You will meet and need to use it in many parts of the exam.

Look at these sentences from the recording.

- *I'd **get wet** in the rain.*
- *We'd all **get to work** in much less time.*
- *Are you **getting the bus**?*
- *I'd have to **get up** earlier.*
- *I wonder how you manage to **get out of bed**.*
- *We'd better **get on** with some work.*

Finish each of the sentences below with an expression from the box. The first one is done for you.

get it back get any notes down	
got to the sports club ~~get wet~~ get out of bed	
get married get on getting off the bus	
get to know her get on get back late	
gets angry get very hot get up late	

1 If you forget your umbrella, you might .*get wet.*.
2 She looks such an interesting person, I'd really like to ....
3 My sister and her boyfriend have decided to ....
4 I am so different from my brother that we really don't ....
5 I shall have to leave without you if you ....
6 Even when her children are very naughty, she never ....
7 The lecturer spoke so fast I couldn't ....
8 We've spent too much time chatting – now we must ....
9 In the winter I find it really difficult to ....
10 When I play squash, I ....
11 I realised I had forgotten my tennis racket when I ....
12 She was in a hurry for school and slipped as she was ....
13 On Sundays I ....
14 I lent that CD to Jenny – I must remember to ....

Part 1

> In the Speaking Test you work with another student.
> In Part 1 you ask and answer questions together.
> This part lasts 2–3 minutes.
> The examiner will ask you to spell a word.

▶▶ Exam tip!

Make sure you know how to ask questions as well as answer them.

 1 Speaking: asking for and giving personal information

a) Imagine you have just moved to a new town. You meet someone of your age and want to find out about the school or college they go to. Write five questions you might ask them in your notebook.

b) Look at the questions below. Are they similar to the questions you wrote? Match the questions (1–7) to the answers (a–g). The first one is done for you.

1   What's your name?   *b*
2   What school do you go to?
3   How long have you been there?
4   Can you spell the first word of your school's name for me, please?
5   How far is the school from your home?
6   How do you get to school?
7   What is your favourite subject?

a)   Usually by bus but sometimes I walk.
b)   Anna Smith.
c)   History.
d)   Parkside Community College. It's in the town centre.
e)   About two kilometres.
f)   Three and a half years.
g)   P-A-R-K-S-I-D-E.

Look carefully at the answers. Are they all complete sentences? Which of them give extra information?

c) Work with a partner. Ask each other the questions in b) above. Try to give some extra information for some of the questions. When you have finished, write the answers you gave in your notebook.

 2 Pronunciation focus: sounds and spelling

It is important to speak as clearly as possible so your partner understands you. Remember that English spelling is not a good rule for pronunciation and the same sound can be spelt in lots of different ways.

a) Listen to the six words below and make sure you can hear the different vowel sounds.

/eə/	/ɑː/	/ɔː/
there	far	your
hair	sharp	call

b) Now listen to some more words and decide which vowel sounds they have.

c) Listen again and repeat each word.

 3 Language focus: spelling

In Part 1, it is important for you to know the alphabet in English as you will be asked to spell something.

a) Work with a partner. One of you is going to write, and the other is going to speak.

Student A: Look at page 92.

Student B: Write down what your partner says in your notebook. When you have finished, show your words to Student A. Are they spelt correctly?

Now change roles.

Student B: Spell the name of of the following countries for your partner.
1   Mexico
2   Russia
3   Turkey
4   Chile
5   Norway

b) Now spell the names of two countries or towns you have visited. Write them in your notebooks and then check them.

Complete the following:

Short answers are usually better than complete sentences, but don't answer questions with just 'Yes' or 'No' – always try to give an extra piece of ....

(If you don' t remember, look at page 45.)

4 ▶ Look at the exam task below.
Work with a different partner.

You imagine you don't know each other. The examiner tells you to ask each other questions to find out some information about each other. Close your books and ask each other at least four of the questions you have practised.
Also, ask each other a spelling question.
Example: *'Can you spell the name of your maths teacher for me?'*

5 ▶ **Language practice: correcting mistakes**

Look at this conversation between Carla and Yoriko. Can you correct their mistakes?

1 What's you called?

2 My name Carla.

3 What school do you go?

4 At the High School.

5 How long you have been there?

6 Since three years.

7 How much far is the school from your home?

8 Three kilometres distance.

9 How are you getting to school?

10 On bus.

Part 2

▶ In Part 2 the examiner gives you some pictures to look at.
▶ You talk about them together.

1 ▶ **Speaking about sports**

Work with a partner. Look at the sports in the pictures below. Talk about:

- your favourite sport
- the sports you dislike
- the equipment you need for the different sports
- how many players are needed
- which are outdoor and which are indoor

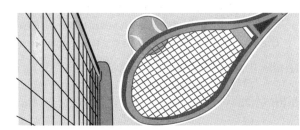

2 ▶ Speaking: making plans

a) Look at the following sentences (1–13) and match them with the descriptions (a–d) below. The first one is done for you.

1 Do you like ...?   *b*
2 I enjoy ...
3 I'd rather ...
4 Do you enjoy ...?
5 What do you want to do?
6 What's your favourite ...?
7 I'd prefer to ...
8 What would you prefer?
9 I'd like to ...
10 Would you like to ...?
11 I like ...
12 My favourite is ...
13 I prefer ...

a) asking what your partner wants to do
b) asking what your partner likes doing
c) saying what you like doing
d) saying what you want to do

b) Read the following conversation between Linda and Julia who are planning a trip to a sports centre. Fill each space with a suitable phrase from the list (a–k) below. The first one is done for you.

Linda: I want to go to a sports club. Black's is good. (**1**) ...*b*... come too? (**2**) .... sports?
Julia: Oh yes. (**3**) .... squash, for example. But really, (**4**) .... sports which you can do outdoors. What about you, (**5**) .... outdoor sports?
Linda: I (**6**) .... most sports, but (**7**) .... tennis.
Julia: What sports can we do at Black's?
Linda: They offer a good range. And there is a swimming pool. But it's rather far away.
Julia: What about Forest's? That's nearer. And they have lots of tennis courts.
Linda: (**8**) .... go to a club with a swimming pool.
Julia: But we'd have to catch a bus to Black's.
Linda: Well, (**9**) ....?
Julia: (**10**) .... You decide.
Linda: OK. (**11**) .... to go to Black's. But I'll pay your bus fare!

a) do you like
b) Would you like to
c) what do you want to do
d) Do you like
e) I prefer
f) I like
g) my favourite is
h) I'd rather
i) I'm not sure
j) enjoy
k) I'd prefer

c) Work with a partner. Plan an afternoon or evening which you will spend at a sports centre. Use the language you have been practising. Can you agree?

  Exam tip!

It doesn't matter if you and your partner can't agree but you must try to.

3 ▶ Vocabulary: places to stay

Work with a partner. How many different places can you think of where you can stay when you go on holiday?

Example: a campsite

> ▶ **Key strategy**
>
> *Complete the following:*
>
> **Listen carefully to what your partner says, so that you can give a ...., like people having a real conversation.**
>
> *(If you don't remember, look at page 46.)*

4 ▶ Look at the exam task. Work with a partner.

You are planning to spend a few days together after your exams. Look at page 148. There are some pictures of places to stay. Decide together which place you are going to stay at. Think about the time of year, the cost, and how you will get there. Ask and answer questions like these:

- Which one do you prefer?
- What can we do there?
- Will it be very expensive?
- What about the others?

Speaking Part 1, Exercise 3

Student A: Spell the names of the following cities for your partner.
1 Germany
2 Australia
3 Egypt
4 Greece
5 Venezuela

Now change roles.

Student A: Write down what your partner says in your notebook. When you have finished, show your words to Student B. Are they spelt correctly?

Part 3

> In Part 3 the examiner gives you and your partner two photos to talk about.
> You talk about your photograph to your partner.

1 ▶ Speaking: describing where things are in a picture

a) Label the numbered parts of the pictures below. Use a dictionary to help you.

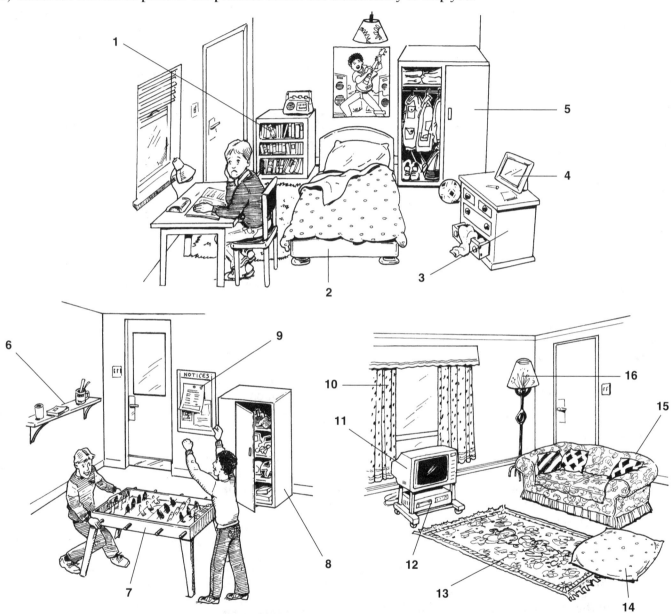

b) Work with a partner. Take turns to ask each other where things and people are in the pictures above. Use the phrases in the box to help you.

at the back	at the front	on one side	on the left	on the right	next to
in one corner	in the other corner	round the table football		by the window	

Example: 'In picture A, where's the desk?'
*   'It's by the window.'*

c) Write four sentences describing where the furniture is in the room you are in now.

2 ▶ Vocabulary: how people feel

a) Look at the words in the box. Which could you use to describe the person in picture A? Which could you use to describe the people in picture B? Which don't fit either?

busy calm noisy excited tired happy
cheerful worried depressed anxious
amused stressed cross unhappy thoughtful
miserable lonely impatient grateful
disappointed astonished

b) Now write sentences about each of the people in the pictures in Exercise 1. Use the language in the box to help you.

Example:
Picture A: He looks bored.

Useful language

He seems ...
He looks ...
He might be ...

3 ▶ ▭ Pronunciation focus: word stress

It is important to put the correct stress on words. This will make it easier for other people to understand you.

Lonely has two syllables – *lone/ly*. We put the stress on the first syllable <u>lone</u>ly.

a) Look at the words below. Which ones have the stress on the first syllable?

grateful   thoughtful   amused   depressed
happy   astonished   worried   jealous
impatient   miserable   excited   annoyed

b) Listen to the recording and check your answers. Mark the main stress in the other words.

c) Listen to the recording again and repeat the words.

4 ▶ Writing: describing where things are in a picture

Work with a partner. Think about the pictures in Exercise 1 but don't look at them. Can you remember where the furniture is in each of the pictures?

Example:
In picture 1, the desk is by the window.

With your partner, write down everything you can remember. When you have finished, look at the pictures to see if you have forgotten anything.

   Key strategy

Complete the following:

Remember to say what is .... in your photograph as well as what things there are in it.

(If you don't remember, look at page 49.)

---

5 ▶ Look at the exam task below. Work with a partner.

Candidate A: look at photograph 2A on page 152.
Candidate B: look at photograph 2B on page 155.

Think about your photograph for a few seconds. Describe it to your partner for about one minute. Tell your partner about these things:

- where you think it is
- what you can see in the picture
- what the people are doing
- why you think they are there
- whether they are interested in what they are doing
- whether they are learning a lot.

▶▶ **Exam tip!**

Don't worry if you don't know a word – try to say it in another way, e.g. if you don't know 'wardrobe', say 'a cupboard for keeping clothes in'.

Part 4

> In Part 4 the examiner asks you to talk to your partner about a particular subject.

> You give your opinion about something and explain what you prefer.

 Speaking about schools

a) Make a list of information about your school. Make sure you include the following:

- number of students in school
- number of students in a class
- number of teachers
- age of students
- subjects studied
- what people from your school do next (go to university / to work etc.)
- extra activities (sports, music, drama, etc.).

b) Now work with a partner. If you go to the same school, do you have the same information? If you go (or went) to different schools, compare your school with your partner's school.

c) What do you think makes a good school? Look at the list below. Decide what is most important and write 1 next to it. Put the rest of the list in order of importance.

- friendly atmosphere
- lots of computers
- hard-working students
- good sports facilities
- modern classrooms
- uniform
- good exam results
- strict teachers
- clear rules

Work with a partner. Compare your lists. Explain why you made your choices.

 Speaking: describing similarities and differences

Look at the three bicycles on the right – they belong to Rosie, Sally and Wendy. With a partner, make two sentences for each one. Use the language patterns in the box to help you.

Example:
Rosie's bicycle is similar to Wendy's.

X is like Y.
X is similar to Y.
X is different from Y.
X is big but Y is small.

Rosie   Sally

Wendy

Do you have a bicycle? Is it like any of the ones in the pictures?

> **Key strategy**
>
> *Complete the following:*
>
> **It's important to give a .... for your opinions – it makes the conversation much more interesting.**
>
> *(If you don't remember, look at page 50.)*

 Look at the exam task below. Work with a partner.

> Tell each other about your school (now or in the past).
> - Which of the photographs looks more like your classes?
> - Would you like to be in the other class?
> - Why / Why not?

▶▶ **Exam tip!**

Don't worry if you can't think of much to say at first. The examiner will help you by asking you questions.

TESTS 3-5

Tests 3, 4 and 5 give you the opportunity to practise what you have learned in Tests 1 and 2.

Test 3 contains **Exam tips!** to help you with each task.

You can use these tests for timed practice, so you get used to doing the tasks under exam conditions.

When you have finished, you will be ready to take the exam with confidence.

Good luck!

TEST 3

Reading

Part 1

Questions 1–5

- Look at the sign in each question.
- Someone asks you what it means.
- Mark the letter next to the correct explanation – **A**, **B**, **C** or **D** – **on your answer sheet**.

> **▶▶ Exam tip!**
>
> Think about the meaning of the whole sign before you choose your answer. The answer with the same words in it as the sign may not be correct – check the other answers too.

Example:

0

DO NOT PARK YOUR CAR BY THESE GATES

A   Parking near these gates is forbidden.

B   The entrance to the car park is through these gates.

C   Do not bring your car into this park.

D   Close these gates after parking your car.

Example answer:

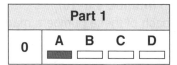

Part 1			
0	A ▓	B ☐	C ☐ D ☐

1

EXCITING NEW RANGE – IMPORTED SILK TIES

A   Sports clothes are on sale here.

B   Foreign ties are available.

C   There are special prices for tourists.

D   We make and sell silk dresses.

2

Job applications to be left at reception not with security guard

A   Give your application form to the receptionist.

B   There is a job available as a security guard.

C   Reception can pass a message to the security guard.

D   If there is no one at reception, speak to the security guard.

3

Please go to Customer
Services on ground floor
if you wish to
exchange goods

A You can try on clothes on the ground floor.

B You can change your money at Customer Services.

C You change things you don't want at Customer Services.

D You pay for everything on the ground floor.

4

OPEN 10 A.M. TUESDAYS
TO ALLOW FOR STAFF
TRAINING.
NORMAL OPENING 8.30.

A The shop assistants are trained on Tuesday mornings.

B The shop assistants leave early on Tuesdays.

C There is a delivery on Tuesday mornings.

D There are interviews for new staff on Tuesday mornings.

5

WAIT OUTSIDE STATION
FOR AIRPORT BUS –
EVERY 15 MINUTES

A The bus to the airport waits here for 15 minutes.

B It takes 15 minutes from the station to the airport.

C The bus waits to collect passengers from the station.

D The airport bus stops regularly at the station.

Part 2

Questions 6–10

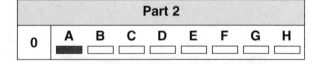 **Exam tip!**

Underline the important
parts of each question.
You can only choose
each text (A–H) once.

- The people below all want to do an English course.
- On the opposite page there are descriptions of eight courses.
- Decide which course (**letters A–H**) would be most suitable for each person or group (**numbers 6–10**).
- For each of these numbers mark the correct letter **on your answer sheet**.

Example answer:

Part 2								
0	A	B	C	D	E	F	G	H
	▉	☐	☐	☐	☐	☐	☐	☐

6  Paolo is good at speaking and understanding English, but he needs to do a full-time course to improve his writing and spelling before he starts a business course next year. He can come to England for one month in December or January.

7  This Spanish family would like to spend two or three weeks attending a part-time language course. The girls are nineteen and eighteen and know quite a lot of English. The parents know very little English.

8 Nikos is fourteen and his sister Anastasia is sixteen. Their parents would like them to spend a month on a language course where they can learn new hobbies and be looked after by their teachers.

9 Mehdi has just finished university and wants to spend some time touring round the world. He would like to do a course for a week or two before he starts his trip as he has never studied English.

10 Dorit is leaving school in June and will start a course to become a tour guide about four months later. Her English is good, but she must get a language qualification before she starts college.

Kinghall English Courses – something for everyone!

A
Activity language learning
For teenagers up to age sixteen with any level of English. Fully-qualified staff and instructors make learning fun and safe. Spend two weeks or a month in small classes, improving your English while you paint, make music, play tennis, volleyball, etc., and take part in many other activities.

B
Family summer school
Classes at all levels for adults (over sixteen) and ten to fifteen-year-olds in the same building. Meet for meals and evening leisure activities. Accommodation in modern flats near the school. A full-day study timetable for one, two or three weeks.

C
Get around in English
This course is aimed at beginners who want to feel comfortable using English to buy tickets, book hotel rooms and make new friends. Although you will spend most of the course simply taking part in conversations, you will work hard and you will be surprised how much progress you make in just two weeks.

D
Examination course 1
For students over sixteen, three-month courses preparing for a certificate recognised by international companies and employers around the world. Full-time courses for students who are prepared to work seriously hard.

E
Examination course 2
For students over sixteen, these courses last six months, and are part-time in the first three months, with a choice of afternoon leisure activities, changing to full-time for the second three months, with increased homework as the examination approaches.

F
Special skills courses
These one, two or three-month courses take place from January to March and are aimed at students who wish to improve particular language skills. Listening, writing, reading and speaking are all offered, together or separately. Students are not advised to take more than two skills in one month.

G
English for tourism
A six-month course for students with some knowledge of the language. The course covers areas such as ticket sales, making reservations and telephone work. Several trips to important English tourist centres are included. A very useful course for people planning to make a career in the travel business.

H
Adults' language breaks
These courses offer serious study during the morning, followed by the opportunity to join short trips to places of interest in the afternoon if you wish. Minimum three weeks, up to six weeks. Minimum age eighteen, all levels from beginners to advanced.

Part 3

Questions 11–20

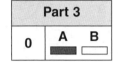 **Exam tip!**

Read the statements first to find out what the text is about.

- Look at the statements about a group of islands.
- Read the text below to decide if each statement is correct or incorrect.
- If it is correct, mark **A on your answer sheet**.
- If it is incorrect, mark **B on your answer sheet**.

Example answer:

	Part 3	
0	A	B
	▬▬	▭

11   St Margaret Island is smaller than St Michael Island.

12   There was no one living on the islands in the 1980s.

13   There are several restaurants on the islands.

14   Flowers are for sale in the island shop.

15   The church is at the top of the highest hill.

16   There is one beach on St Michael Island where it is safe to swim.

17   It is possible to take a boat trip on a Saturday.

18   There is a fee for landing on the islands.

19   The journey to the islands lasts half an hour.

20   There is an exhibition centre on the islands.

Ferndig Islands

Three miles across the water from the town of Blascott lies the group of islands known as the Ferndigs. The main island is St Michael. Separated by a narrow channel of water is St Michael's little sister, St Margaret. People first lived on these islands 1500 years ago. By the 1950s the population had gone down to below twenty and in 1960 the last person left the islands. But in 1991 two families moved back and since then more people have followed. Tourists now visit regularly to enjoy the beautiful scenery.

Visit the one shop on the islands which sells butter, cheese and bread produced by the families who live there. The produce is also taken by boat to restaurants in Blascott where it can be enjoyed by visitors to the area. Perhaps more interestingly, a range of perfumes are made from the wild flowers and herbs which grow on the island and can be bought in the shop. They are produced mainly for export and are very special. So a visit to the shop is a must!

St Michael Island is easily explored on foot but, in the interests of safety, visitors are requested to keep to the main footpaths. From where the boat lands, walk along the cliff until you reach a steep path signposted to the church. When you get there, it is worth spending a moment in this lovely old building. Carry on along the same path which continues to climb to the highest point on the island. There is a wonderful view from here along the coastline. If it is warm, you may like to finish your day relaxing on the beach. Priory Beach on the eastern side of the island is safe for swimming. Sandtop Bay on the western side is the other sandy beach but swimming is not advised here.

It is possible to hire a boat to cross to the islands or you can take one of the boat trips which depart from Blascott harbour in summer, Monday–Friday. The islands are always open to visitors apart from on Sundays. Buy a ticket for a boat trip from the kiosk in Blascott harbour. The charge for landing on the islands is included in the ticket but, if you take your own boat, remember to take some money. The crossing takes thirty minutes and boats run every fifteen minutes.

Before you set off on a trip, visit the exhibition centre which tells the history of the islands and gives information about birds and wildlife you may see when you get there.

Part 4

Questions 21–25

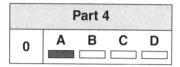

Exam tip!

The text will be about opinions and attitudes as well as information.

- Read the text and questions below.
- For each question, mark the letter next to the correct answer – **A**, **B**, **C** or **D** – on **your answer sheet**.

Example answer:

Part 4				
0	**A** ▉	**B** ☐	**C** ☐	**D** ☐

My name is James, I'm fourteen, and I moved to this town with my family three months ago. My parents lived here when they were young, but my brother and I didn't know anyone here except a few relatives we'd met on visits. When I started school, one of my cousins, Sophie, who was in my class, was very friendly for the first week and I was happy to have a friend in a strange place. Then, for no reason, she stopped talking to me and I felt very hurt and lonely for several weeks. In the end I made some more friends and since I got to know them, I've been fine. Now Sophie is having a disco party for her birthday next week and she has invited me. I don't want to go. My brother says he heard someone say she only asked me because her parents said she had to. But my Mum and Dad say it would be rude not to accept. Some of my new friends are invited, too. How can I show Sophie that she can't behave so badly towards me without causing a family quarrel?

21   What is the writer trying to do in the text?

   A   explain a problem

   B   describe a family

   C   offer advice

   D   refuse an invitation

22   What can we learn from reading the text?

   A   Sophie's opinion of her cousin

   B   what the writer feels about Sophie

   C   what Sophie's friends feel about her

   D   how the writer feels about Sophie's friends

[Turn over

23 At the beginning of term, Sophie's behaviour made the writer feel

    A embarrassed.

    B unhappy.

    C grateful.

    D surprised.

24 The writer wants Sophie to realise

    A that he still hasn't forgiven her.

    B that her friends think she behaved rudely.

    C that his parents dislike her.

    D that she has fewer friends than he has.

25 Which of these is written in answer?

    A   Ask your friends to come with you and we can all have a good time together.

    B   Why not go to the party and ask Sophie why she stopped being friendly? At least everyone will know what's happening.

    C   Please phone my parents and explain the situation to them, so that they'll stop worrying.

    D   What about cooking a meal with Sophie and inviting all your relatives? That will be a good way to stop them quarrelling.

Part 5

Questions 26–35

 **Exam tip!**

Write the words in the spaces. When you have finished, read through the text and check they sound right.

- Read the text below and choose the correct word for each space.
- For each question, mark the letter next to the correct word – **A**, **B**, **C** or **D** – on your answer sheet.

Example answer:

Part 5				
0	A ■	B ☐	C ☐	D ☐

Weather

Weather influences the lives **(0)** .... everyone. The climate of any country depends on its position on Earth, its **(26)** .... from the sea and how high it is. In countries which have sea all **(27)** .... them, like Britain and New Zealand, winters are mild and summers are cool. There is not a huge change from one season to **(28)** .... Countries near the Equator have hot weather all year with some **(29)** .... rain, except in deserts where it rains **(30)** .... little. Above the desert there are no clouds in the sky so the **(31)** .... of the sun can easily warm the ground during the day but it gets very cold at night. People are always **(32)** .... in unusual weather and pictures of tornadoes, for example, are shown on television. Strong winds and rain can **(33)** .... a lot of damage to buildings and in spite of modern **(34)** .... of weather forecasting they can **(35)** .... surprise us.

0	**A** of	**B** from	**C** by	**D** to
26	**A** distance	**B** space	**C** depth	**D** length
27	**A** through	**B** beside	**C** around	**D** near
28	**A** next	**B** another	**C** later	**D** other
29	**A** hard	**B** large	**C** heavy	**D** great
30	**A** not	**B** quite	**C** more	**D** very
31	**A** heat	**B** fire	**C** light	**D** temperature
32	**A** attracted	**B** interested	**C** keen	**D** excited
33	**A** make	**B** happen	**C** have	**D** cause
34	**A** jobs	**B** tools	**C** methods	**D** plans
35	**A** yet	**B** still	**C** already	**D** ever

Writing

Part 1

Questions 1–5

- Here are some sentences about visiting the doctor.
- For each question, finish the second sentence so that it means the same as the first.
- The second sentence is started for you. **Write only the missing words on your answer sheet.**
- You may use this page for any rough work.

Example: I don't visit the doctor very often.

I hardly .*ever visit the doctor.*...

1   I last visited the doctor a year ago.

I haven't visited the doctor ....

2   When I phoned, the receptionist asked which doctor I wanted to see.

When I phoned, the receptionist asked 'Which doctor ....?'

3   I like Dr Simmonds better than Dr Turner.

I prefer ....

4   Today the doctors are busier than usual.

The doctors aren't usually as ....

5   Luckily, the waiting room has lots of magazines to read.

Luckily, in the waiting room there ....

Part 2

Questions 6–15

▶▶ Exam tip!

Give exactly the information you are asked for but remember it's not necessary to write full sentences.

- You are studying in Britain.
- A clothes shop is offering students a discount card.
- Look at the form and answer each question.
- **Write your answers on your answer sheet.**
- You may use this page for any rough work.

BEST BUY CLOTHES STORE

Upper Station Road
Northwood
NW4 8HU
UK

Get one of our discount cards now!

Full name: (**6**) ....

Home address (including country): (**7**) ....

....

Date of birth (day / month / year): (**8**) ....

Sex: (**9**) ....

Nationality: (**10**) ....

How much time do you spend shopping for clothes each week? (**11**) ....

....

On which day(s) of the week do you usually go shopping? (**12**) ....

....

What clothes do you usually wear? (**13**) ....

What is your favourite colour? (**14**) ....

Who do you usually go shopping with? (**15**) ....

....

Part 3

When you finish writing, read through your letter carefully to check for any mistakes.

Question 16

- You have just come back from a holiday.
- Now you are writing a letter to an English-speaking friend about the holiday.
- Tell your friend about where you went, say what you did there and describe the accommodation you stayed in.
- **Finish the letter on your answer sheet, using about 100 words.**

Dear . . . . . ,

I want to tell you about my holiday. ....

....

> You must write your answers on
> the separate answer sheet.

TEST 3, WRITING PART 3

Part 1

> ▶▶ **Exam tip!**
>
> **Use the pictures to help you understand what you will hear.**

Questions 1–7

- There are seven questions in this Part.
- For each question there are four pictures and a short recording.
- You will hear each recording twice.
- For each question, look at the pictures and listen to the recording.
- Choose the correct picture and put a tick (✓) in the box below it.

Example: Which train will the woman catch?

A ☐   B ☐   C ✓   D ☐

1 Which is the woman's house?

A ☐   B ☐   C ☐   D ☐

2 Where is the shopping list?

A ☐   B ☐   C ☐   D ☐

[Turn over

3 Which wedding present has the man bought?

A ☐   B ☐   C ☐   D ☐

4 How did the man get home?

A ☐   B ☐   C ☐   D ☐

5 What will the girl buy at the shop?

A ☐   B ☐   C ☐   D ☐

6 Which is the man's sister?

A ☐   B ☐   C ☐   D ☐

7 Which poster are they looking at?

A ☐   B ☐   C ☐   D ☐

Part 2

Questions 8–13

Exam tip!

The questions are in the same order as the information you hear, so if you can't answer a question at first, leave it and do the others.

- Look at the questions for this Part.
- You will hear a successful fashion designer talking about his career.
- Put a tick (✓) in the correct box for each question.

8 How well did the speaker do at school?

    A ☐ He was an average student.

    B ☐ His parents helped him.

    C ☐ He got into trouble.

    D ☐ He had problems passing exams.

9 What did he do when he left school?

    A ☐ He got a job to earn a lot of money.

    B ☐ He did a business course.

    C ☐ He went to art college.

    D ☐ He studied to pass some exams.

10 What did he learn from his part-time job?

    A ☐ how to sew

    B ☐ how to design cheap clothes

    C ☐ how clothes are made

    D ☐ how to run a large business

11 When did he go to London?

    A ☐ at the age of seventeen

    B ☐ after working for an Italian company

    C ☐ as soon as he had enough money

    D ☐ when he won a prize

12 How long did he stay in Milan?

    A ☐ three months

    B ☐ nine months

    C ☐ one year

    D ☐ three years

13 Why did he have difficulties in New York?

    A ☐ He wanted to be nearer his home.

    B ☐ The work was more stressful than he had expected.

    C ☐ He quickly became very tired.

    D ☐ He could not start a company there.

Part 3

▶▶ **Exam tip!**

Use the words around the spaces to help you decide what kind of answer is needed.

Questions 14–19

- Look at the notes about a shopping centre.
- Some information is missing.
- You will hear a tour guide talking to some tourists about a visit to the shopping centre.
- For each question, fill in the missing information in the numbered space.

Visit to shopping centre

Bank is on the (**14**) ....

Get a (**15**) .... from the newsagent.

Restaurant is opposite the (**16**) .... in the main square.

Snack bar next to the (**17**) .... closes

at (**18**) ....

Meet outside shop called (**19**) ....

Part 4

Questions 20–25

▶▶ Exam tip!

Look carefully at the verbs in the statements (e.g. *decided*, *agrees*, *persuades*) because they are all very important in helping you choose the answer.

- Look at the six statements for this Part.
- You will hear a conversation between a girl, Alice, and a boy, Sam, about a play their school is doing called *Romeo and Juliet*.
- Decide if you think each statement is correct or incorrect.
- If you think it is correct, put a tick (✓) in the box under **A** for **YES**. If you think it is not correct, put a tick (✓) in the box under **B** for **NO**.

		A YES	B NO
20	They are going to have the practice outdoors today.	☐	☐
21	Sam has decided he no longer wants to be Romeo.	☐	☐
22	Alice agrees with Miss Hayes about Sam's voice.	☐	☐
23	Sam agrees that Alice should speak to Miss Hayes about the problem.	☐	☐
24	Alice persuades Sam to take a smaller part in the play.	☐	☐
25	Someone is needed to produce the scenery.	☐	☐

Part 1

General conversation: saying who you are, asking for and giving personal information, spelling

▶▶ **Exam tip!**

Try to have a real conversation with your partner, as if you are getting to know a new friend.

You imagine you don't know each other. The examiner directs you to ask each other questions to find out some information about each other.

Ask each other at least four of these questions:

- What's your name?
- How long have you been studying English?
- Where do you study?
- How many students are there in your class?
- How many hours a week do you have English?
- Can you spell your teacher's surname for me, please?

Part 2

Simulated situation: exchanging opinions, saying what you think other people would like

▶▶ **Exam tip!**

Speak to your partner, not the examiner, and listen to what each other says.

The examiner gives you both a picture. You do a task together.

You are going to buy a present for your teacher who is in hospital after a road accident. Look at page 149. There is a picture of your teacher and some of the things you might buy. Decide together what you are going to buy. Think about what your teacher can do and what he might enjoy. Ask and answer questions like these:

- What would he enjoy?
- What would amuse him?
- What would be interesting for him?
- Would that be too tiring?
- Do you think he already has one?

Part 3

Responding to photographs: describing situations and settings

▶▶ **Exam tip!**

Don't worry if you don't know the name of something – describe it instead.

You take turns to tell each other about a photograph.

Candidate A: look at photograph 3A on page 153.
Candidate B: look at photograph 3B on page 155.

Think about your photograph for a few seconds. Describe it to your partner for about one minute. Tell your partner about these things:

- what kind of place it is
- who do you think the people are
- what sport people are doing
- whether they are enjoying what they are doing
- why they are doing it.

Part 4

General conversation about the photographs: talking about likes, dislikes and preferences

▶▶ **Exam tip!**

If you agree or disagree, don't just say Yes or No – explain why.

The examiner asks you to talk to your partner. You give your opinion about something and explain what you prefer.

Tell each other about sports you enjoy doing or watching (now or in the past). Use these ideas.

- Say if you like watersports.
- Say what other sports you like.
- Say if you enjoy sports competitions and why.
- Say if you prefer watching sport or doing it and why.

TEST 4

PAPER 1 Reading and Writing Test (1 hour 30 minutes)

Reading

Part 1

Questions 1–5

- Look at the sign in each question.
- Someone asks you what it means.
- Mark the letter next to the correct explanation – **A**, **B**, **C** or **D** – **on your answer sheet**.

Example:

0
> **DO NOT PARK YOUR CAR BY THESE GATES**

A Parking near these gates is forbidden.

B The entrance to the car park is through these gates.

C Do not bring your car into this park.

D Close these gates after parking your car.

Example answer:

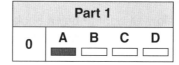

1
> **For repairs when shop is closed leave locked bicycles outside. Put keys in letter box.**

A You can leave your bicycle here for repair even if the shop is closed.

B We will send you a letter when your bicycle is repaired.

C You should leave us the keys so that we can lock your bicycle.

D We will leave your bicycle outside when we have repaired it.

2
> **Do not touch china. Ask shop assistant to serve you.**

A Put the china back in the right place after looking at it.

B If you want to pick up the china, find an assistant to help you.

C Pay for the china before you touch it.

D If no shop assistant is available, take your china to the service desk.

3

ANY LOST PROPERTY LEFT HERE AFTER TWO WEEKS IS SOLD

A   We charge a fine for lost property not collected within two weeks.

B   We give lost property away if it is not collected after two weeks.

C   We will look after your property for two weeks if you pay a fee.

D   We keep things people have lost for a maximum of two weeks.

4

Choose a pair of gloves
FREE
when you buy a coat today

A   All gloves are at reduced prices today.

B   You are given some gloves if you buy a coat today.

C   We have gloves to match the coats we sell.

D   You can get a discount on a coat if you buy some gloves today.

5

PHOTOCOPYING
Serve yourself
Count number of copies
Pay assistant at till on way out

A   Check you have the correct number of photocopies before leaving.

B   Put your money in the photocopier before you start to use it.

C   Tell an assistant how many photocopies you need.

D   Do your photocopying and pay for it when you leave.

Part 2

Questions 6–10

- The people below all want to buy a book.
- On the opposite page there are descriptions of eight books.
- Decide which book (**letters A–H**) would be most suitable for each person (**numbers 6–10**).
- For each of these numbers mark the correct letter **on your answer sheet**.

Example answer:

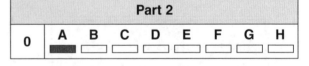

Part 2							
0	A	B	C	D	E	F	G	H

6

Jan is sixteen and she loves shopping for clothes and reading stories about people and things in the news. She wants to read some entertaining light fiction.

7

Paul is nineteen and is very keen on sport. He doesn't enjoy fiction much, but does like reading about the lives of sporting heroes of the past.

8 Susan is eighteen and enjoys good writing. She would like something which offers information as well as entertainment. She's interested in history and plans to travel round Europe this summer.

9 Michael is twenty-three, a computer expert, whose interests include travel and sport. He has to go abroad for work and wants a novel to read on his journey with plenty of action and excitement.

10 Sonia is twenty-four and works for an international airline. She enjoys love stories of the past, especially if they contain descriptions of beautiful houses, clothes and parties.

A ### The Beauty by Sophie Harper
The lovely Emmaline Barton was an American girl who came to Europe in the nineteenth century and won the hearts of young men in every great city. This entertaining novel takes us into a well-imagined world of palaces and gardens and shows us the wonderful silk dresses, the bright lights and the sparkling eyes.

B ### European Hotels and Guesthouses by Andrew Peters
A very clear and helpful book which lists accommodation in most main European cities, with brief descriptions and a good price guide. Its small size makes it easy for the traveller to pack, and the organisation of the information makes it quick and easy to use.

C ### Getting There by Will Jenkins
This is the first part of the autobiography of the international gymnastics star. He writes his own story well, hiding none of the difficulties that he had to face and he brings to life the heartaches, as well as the joys, of young sportsmen and women who really want to find success.

D ### Trains and Boats and Planes by Rachel Bryant
Sometimes funny, sometimes exciting, occasionally sad, this beautifully-written little book describes the adventures of a group of American students who spent a year working and studying in Europe. There are lively descriptions of some of the great cities and their inhabitants, past and present.

E ### What People Wore by Annabel Stoneman
An extremely interesting history of clothes, written by a history teacher. It will be a very useful book for anyone who needs to design clothes for the theatre or who is interested in the everyday lives of people in the past. There are not many pictures, but lots of detailed notes.

F ### Future Pop by Terry Orpen
The pop music industry has changed enormously in the past few years. With electronics and computers in the studio and at concerts, what is the future for the human musician? This book is by one of the top performers of computer pop music and he discusses the way it will probably develop in the future.

G ### Goal Posts by Simon Brown
A very well-written and fast-moving adventure story, set in the imagined world of international football stars. The matches are well described, as well as the problems of the players as they fight for their careers, on and off the pitch. A great read for sports fans.

H ### The Fashion House by Julia Davis
This amusing novel is just right for reading on holiday. It reveals the lives and loves of the designers, models and customers of a famous fashion house. It's written by a former model and gives away many of the modern fashion world's secrets.

Part 3

Questions 11–20

- Look at the statements about a holiday in Tasmania, an island off the south coast of Australia.
- Read the text below to decide if each statement is correct or incorrect.
- If it is correct, mark **A on your answer sheet**.
- If it is incorrect, mark **B on your answer sheet**.

Example answer:

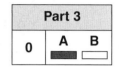

Part 3		
0	A	B

11 There are few traffic jams in Tasmania.

12 There are several buses every day on most routes.

13 It is essential to reserve accommodation in advance.

14 There is a limit on the number of hotel tickets you can buy.

15 Ruby Hotels are the cheapest.

16 Taz Hotel tickets can only be used in Taz Hotels.

17 The most attractive scenery you see on the second day is by Russell Falls.

18 The third day is spent in the car.

19 There are good views of Cradle Mountain from the edges of Dove Lake.

20 The trip finishes where it started.

See Tasmania!

Rich in an old world charm and with magnificent National Parks, Tasmania is well covered by a good road network. Light traffic and wonderful views make driving these roads a pleasure. Though the bus system is reliable, on many routes services may only run once daily. So hire a car and see this beautiful and interesting island at your own speed.

There is a variety of places to stay, and although booking is strongly advised, particularly at peak holiday times, it should not be too difficult to arrange things as you go, if you prefer. We sell you a set of Taz Hotel Pass vouchers and Tasmania is yours. The Taz Hotel Pass offers the visitor a simple and convenient way to stay anywhere in Australia. Each hotel ticket is paid for in advance and is for one night's accommodation. There is no maximum or minimum number of hotel tickets you can buy, and we will give you your money back on unused tickets, less a small administrative charge. Taz Hotels are divided into simple colour categories with Ruby being the most basic and Diamond representing the highest quality. We recommend that you buy a mixture of tickets as we cannot give you your money back if you use a higher value ticket when staying at a lower value hotel. If you travel to an area where Taz have no hotels, then we will find other reasonably-priced accommodation for you in exchange for your Taz tickets.

Here is the planned route for our holiday in Tasmania:

Day 1: Arrive Hobart airport, pick up your car and spend some time in the capital, perhaps driving up to the Old Signal Station on Mount Nelson.

Day 2: Drive through the Derwent Valley, stopping at Russell Falls. Later the scenery becomes even more amazing as you pass Lake St Clair National Park. Spend the night in the fishing town of Strahan.

Day 3: We take you on a half-day cruise from Strahan on the famous Gordon River. Then set off for a leisurely drive to Cradle Mountain National Park.

Day 4: Enjoy the wild beauty of the Park. Go fishing or horse-riding. Or walk around beautiful Dove Lake, from where there are wonderful views of the mountain itself.

Day 5: Explore the fascinating country towns as you drive north and along the coast to Launceston, Tasmania's second largest city.

Day 6: A pleasant drive through peaceful countryside to Hobart. On route, you pass the charming towns of Ross and Oatlands. Return to the airport in time for your flight.

Part 4

Questions 21–25

- Read the text and questions below.
- For each question, mark the letter next to the correct answer – **A**, **B**, **C** or **D** – on **your answer sheet**.

Example answer:

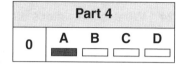

	Part 4			
	A	B	C	D
0	▆▆▆	☐	☐	☐

There is a story going round at the moment about a well-known journalist who went to interview Jack Parrish at a smart New York restaurant. The journalist was late, but fortunately, when he arrived, he found the great man was not yet there. After fifteen minutes, a waiter approached him. 'There's some young man at the door who says he's supposed to be having lunch with you. I think he's trying to be funny, because he says his name is Jack Parrish!'

But of course it was. The twenty-four-year-old is becoming famous for the fact that he doesn't look like the owner of one of the world's most successful computer companies. His manner is polite, his voice is quiet and his clothes are clearly not expensive. Two years ago, when he started his own company, no one had heard of him. Friends say that he hasn't changed at all. He hasn't even moved out of his parents' house. So what does he do with his money? It's all in his company. But some people in the computer world are getting nervous – and they are right. It won't be long before someone in another company picks up the phone to hear that quiet voice saying that he's the new boss.

21 Someone could find out from this text

    A how Jack Parrish runs his business.

    B what Jack Parrish said in an interview.

    C how to get a job in Jack Parrish's company.

    D what the writer thinks Jack Parrish will do next.

22 What is the writer trying to do in the text?

    A say how to make a lot of money

    B give some information about a businessman

    C give some information about a journalist

    D explain how to interview successful people

23 The waiter thought the young man at the door of the restaurant

    A was a journalist.

    B was behaving rudely.

    C was not as old as he said he was.

    D was pretending to be someone else.

24 What is the writer's attitude to Jack Parrish?

    A He is more important than he appears.

    B He is a good example for young people.

    C He should be more careful how he runs his business.

    D He would be an interesting person to work for.

25 Which of these headlines does the writer expect to see soon?

A

Too much success too fast – was that the end of Parrish's luck?

B

Jack Parrish doesn't worry about money – he gives it away to old friends

C

And the new owner of our top computer company is Jack Parrish!

D

SPEND, SPEND, SPEND –
how Jack furnishes his
new million-dollar home

Part 5

Questions 26–35

- Read the text below and choose the correct word for each space.
- For each question, mark the letter next to the correct word – **A, B, C** or **D** – **on your answer sheet**.

Example answer:

Part 5				
0	A ▃▃	B ☐	C ☐	D ☐

English around the world

English is the first language of (0) .... people in countries outside the United Kingdom. When you (26) .... speakers of English from around the world, you (27) .... notice that they do not all speak in the same way. There are also some (28) .... in the words they use, including the names of (29) .... objects that are part of everyone's daily life. But although pronunciation and (30) .... are not the same everywhere, it is interesting that English speakers (31) .... opposite sides of the world can understand (32) .... other quite easily. It does not seem to (33) .... where they learnt the language. And of course this is one reason why speakers of other languages are keen (34) .... learning English too. If you know English, you are more (35) .... to be able to study or work in all sorts of exciting places, such as the United States or Australia.

0	**A** many	**B** much	**C** most	**D** more
26	**A** recognise	**B** meet	**C** find	**D** attend
27	**A** originally	**B** strangely	**C** curiously	**D** immediately
28	**A** mistakes	**B** corrections	**C** changes	**D** differences
29	**A** common	**B** popular	**C** favourite	**D** general
30	**A** reading	**B** composition	**C** dictation	**D** vocabulary
31	**A** of	**B** in	**C** from	**D** at
32	**A** each	**B** one	**C** the	**D** some
33	**A** mind	**B** care	**C** matter	**D** worry
34	**A** by	**B** on	**C** to	**D** for
35	**A** likely	**B** probably	**C** possibly	**D** luckily

Writing

Part 1

Questions 1–5

- Here are some sentences about a restaurant.
- For each question, finish the second sentence so that it means the same as the first.
- The second sentence is started for you. **Write only the missing words on your answer sheet.**
- You may use this page for any rough work.

Example: We've got a new restaurant in our town.

There *is a new restaurant in our town.*...

1 The building was formerly a shoe shop.

The building used ....

2 I still haven't been to it.

I haven't ....

3 'Do you want to go there for lunch tomorrow?' asked Philip.

Philip asked us ....

4 But I couldn't accept his invitation.

But I wasn't ....

5 My lunch break is too short.

My lunch break isn't ....

Part 2

Questions 6–15

- You want to join a sports centre.
- The sports centre gives you an application form to complete.
- Look at the form and answer each question.
- **Write your answers on your answer sheet.**
- You may use this page for any rough work.

Northend Sports Centre

Long Lane, Coalport
CP2 4NL
UK

Application for Membership

Full name: (**6**) ....

Age: (**7**) ....

Sex: (**8**) ....

Nationality: (**9**) ....

What sports do you take part in at present? (**10**) ....

....

Please describe how well you play your favourite sport. (**11**) ....

....

How often do you do sport? (**12**) ....

At what time of day and on which day(s) of the week do you prefer to do sport? (**13**) ....

....

What new sport would you like to start? (**14**) ....

Home address (including country): (**15**) ....

....

Part 3

Question 16

- You are going to spend a month with a family in England.
- Now you are writing a letter to the family to introduce yourself to them.
- Tell them about your work or school, describe some of your hobbies and interests and say what you hope to do while you are in England.
- **Finish the letter on your answer sheet, using about 100 words.**

Dear . . . . . ,

I'm writing to introduce myself to you before we meet. ....

....

> You must write your answers on
> the separate answer sheet.

Part 1

Questions 1–7

- There are seven questions in this Part.
- For each question there are four pictures and a short recording.
- You will hear each recording twice.
- For each question, look at the pictures and listen to the recording.
- Choose the correct picture and put a tick (✓) in the box below it.

Example: Which train will the woman catch?

A ☐   B ☐   C ✓   D ☐

1   Which job does the woman do now?

A ☐   B ☐   C ☐   D ☐

2   Where was the accident?

A ☐   B ☐   C ☐   D ☐

[Turn over

3 Where is the car park?

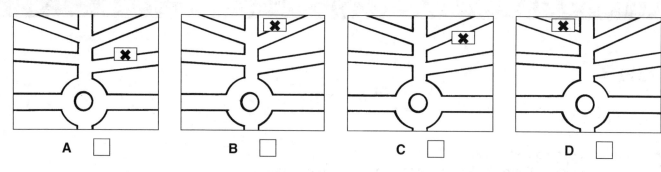

A ☐   B ☐   C ☐   D ☐

4 Which date is Brian's birthday?

A ☐   B ☐   C ☐   D ☐

5 What has the girl hurt?

A ☐   B ☐   C ☐   D ☐

6 Which are the new curtains?

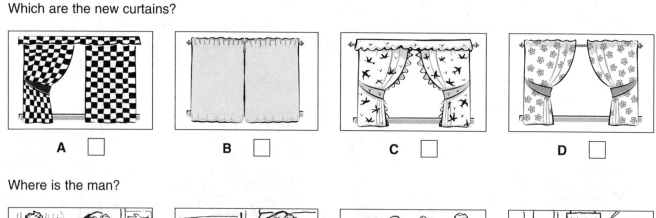

A ☐   B ☐   C ☐   D ☐

7 Where is the man?

A ☐   B ☐   C ☐   D ☐

Part 2

Questions 8–13

- Look at the questions for this Part.
- You will hear part of a radio programme called *What's On*.
- Put a tick (✓) in the correct box for each question.

8 The competition this year is to find the best

    A ☐ actor.

    B ☐ musician.

    C ☐ dancer.

    D ☐ singer.

9 You can enter the competition if you

    A ☐ have won one of the prizes before.

    B ☐ live less than five miles from the city centre.

    C ☐ phone any time after Saturday.

    D ☐ send your entry by post.

10 To find out more about the theatre group you should phone

    A ☐ the radio station.

    B ☐ Saint Paul's School.

    C ☐ the secretary of the group.

    D ☐ the theatre.

11 What is different about the arrangements at the sports hall this week?

    A ☐ The closing time is later than usual.

    B ☐ There are more lessons than normal.

    C ☐ All activities must be booked in advance.

    D ☐ It is not possible to hire the football pitch.

12 What information are we given about the new swimming pool?

    A ☐ It will open next month.

    B ☐ It will be free for one week.

    C ☐ It is bigger than the old one.

    D ☐ It will be open sooner than expected.

13 What are we told about the rock group *Switch*?

    A ☐ They have been popular for four years.

    B ☐ They were all born in Westfield.

    C ☐ They are doing two concerts in Westfield.

    D ☐ They all live in Westfield.

Part 3

Questions 14–19

- Look at the notes about a city walk.
- Some information is missing.
- You will hear someone talking about the city of Cork.
- For each question, fill in the missing information in the numbered space.

Cork

The population is (**14**) ....

Drivers find the number of (**15**) .... confusing.

St Patrick Street – on one side are old buildings, on other side are

(**16**) .... and shops.

Market – (**17**) .... and fruit are recommended today.

Café in the (**18**) .... is good for lunch.

Public Museum is closed on (**19**) ....

Part 4

Questions 20–25

- Look at the six statements for this Part.
- You will hear a conversation between a woman, Kim, and a man, Rob, who live in the same block of flats.
- Decide if you think each statement is correct or incorrect.
- If you think it is correct, put a tick (✓) in the box under **A** for **YES**. If you think it is not correct, put a tick (✓) in the box under **B** for **NO**.

		A YES	B NO
20	Kim gave a party last night.	☐	☐
21	Rob could hear music from Kim's flat.	☐	☐
22	Rob apologises for disturbing Kim's visitors.	☐	☐
23	Rob plays music when he has visitors.	☐	☐
24	Kim dislikes working in silence.	☐	☐
25	Kim prefers to work during the day.	☐	☐

Part 1

General conversation: saying who you are, asking for and giving personal information, spelling

You imagine you don't know each other. The examiner directs you to ask each other questions to find out some information about each other.

Ask each other at least four of these questions:

- What's your name?
- Can you tell me about your family?
- Are you the oldest, the youngest or in the middle?
- Where exactly do you live?
- How long does it take you to get to school?
- Can you spell the name of your street for me, please?

Part 2

Simulated situation: exchanging information and giving opinions

The examiner gives you both a picture. You do a task together.

You are planning to go out with your classmates for a meal. Look at page 150. Decide together where to go to eat. Ask and answer questions like these:

- Which place would people prefer?
- Is it better to have the meal indoors or outdoors?
- What type of food do they have there?

Part 3

Responding to photographs: describing where people and animals are and what they are doing

You take turns to tell each other about a photograph.

Candidate A: look at photograph 4A on page 153.
Candidate B: look at photograph 4B on page 156.

Think about your photograph for a few seconds. Describe it to your partner for about one minute. Tell your partner about these things:

- what kind of place it is
- what part of the world it might be
- what animals and people there are
- how the people are dressed
- what they are doing.

Part 4

General conversation about the photographs: talking about likes, dislikes and preferences

The examiner asks you to talk to your partner. You give your opinion about something and explain what you prefer.

Tell each other about animals you like. Use these ideas.

- Say if you like horses.
- Say if you have ever been horse-riding. Where?
- Say if you would like to. Explain why / why not.
- Say if you have any pets at home.
- Say what other animals you like.
- Say if you know of any unusual pets.

TEST 5

Reading

Part 1

Questions 1–5

- Look at the sign in each question.
- Someone asks you what it means.
- Mark the letter next to the correct explanation – **A, B, C** or **D** – **on your answer sheet**.

Example:

0

> **DO NOT PARK YOUR CAR BY THESE GATES**

A   Parking near these gates is forbidden.

B   The entrance to the car park is through these gates.

C   Do not bring your car into this park.

D   Close these gates after parking your car.

Example answer:

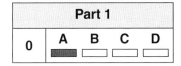

Part 1			
	A	B	C	D
0	▮	☐	☐	☐

1

> **Students arriving late must sign their names in this book before going to class**

A   Students will not be allowed to enter their class if they are late.

B   Students have to put their names in their books before going to class.

C   Students should sign their names in this book if they expect to be late.

D   Students who are late should not go to class before signing this book.

2

> **This entrance is closed today. Use entrance at back of building beside car park.**

A   After today the entrance to the building will be at the back.

B   Cars should be parked at the back of the building not at the front.

C   For today only, you should enter the building from the back.

D   There are two entrances to the building which you can use today.

3

Check with a waiter before sitting down as some tables are reserved

A Ask a waiter which tables are available.

B Ask a waiter if you want to reserve a table.

C It is essential to reserve a table before you arrive.

D It is advisable to find a table before you order your meal.

4

PARENTS ARE REMINDED THAT THIS IS **NOT** A PLAYGROUND – **PLEASE KEEP CHILDREN OFF SCULPTURES!**

A Families can only watch sports events in this park.

B Children must not climb on the sculptures.

C Some of the sculptures are unsuitable for children.

D Only children are allowed in the park.

5

PASSENGERS FOR INTERNATIONAL FLIGHTS – CHECK LUGGAGE IN HERE

A Passengers arriving from abroad must check in their luggage here.

B Travellers from other countries have to check in their own luggage here.

C If you have checked in your luggage, you must wait here for your flight.

D This is where you check in your luggage if you are going abroad.

Part 2

Questions 6–10

- The people below all want to visit a museum in the Kington area.
- On the opposite page there are descriptions of eight museums.
- Decide which museum (**letters A–H**) would be most suitable for each person or family (**numbers 6–10**).
- For each of these numbers mark the correct letter **on your answer sheet**.

Example answer:

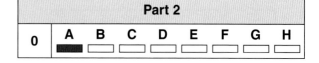

Part 2								
0	A	B	C	D	E	F	G	H
	■	☐	☐	☐	☐	☐	☐	☐

6

Tina is going to art college soon. She wants to spend an afternoon looking at some modern art. She would like to have lunch and buy some art books.

7

Karen needs to buy a special present for a friend and wants to get her some jewellery or pottery made locally. She can only go shopping after five o'clock in the evening.

8 Stefan has just moved to Kington. He would like to find out more about life in the area over the last hundred years. He is only free on Saturdays.

9 Gareth and Sue want to spend Sunday outdoors. Their children want to learn about how people used to live in the past. The family are looking for somewhere which has a playground.

10 Jack is studying art and is particularly interested in the development of painting over the last three hundred years. He is free every afternoon and would like to stop and have a snack in the museum.

Museums and galleries around Kington

A Most of the machines in this interesting museum are indoors but some of the larger farming equipment is outside. A lot of the machines still work and you can try using them. It is especially suitable for school groups and families and is open Monday to Saturday from 10 a.m. till 6 p.m.

B This museum changes its exhibitions regularly. At the moment it is showing paintings by local artists who all live in the area. The excellent bookshop and café are above the gallery. The café is open for lunch from 12 till 2.30 and the gallery and bookshop from 11 till 6 every day.

C The Kington area was once very important industrially and this museum tells the history of the local industries of shipbuilding and pottery. There is a large car park at the front and a playground at the back. The museum is open Monday–Friday from 10–5.

D All the exhibits in this attractive little museum were produced in the region over the last 100 years. There is a good range of jewellery, clothes and pictures for sale all produced in Kington. The museum is open Thursday–Sunday from 2 p.m. till 9 p.m. and the tearoom from 2 p.m. till 5 p.m.

E The best art collection in the area is here and there is a separate room for each century, including a small one for twentieth-century paintings. There is a shop selling posters, postcards and cards. The coffee shop is open for lunch and afternoon tea from midday Tuesday–Saturday. The museum is open from 11 a.m. till 7 p.m. Tuesday–Saturday.

F This museum shows family life in Kington during the twentieth century. There are rooms furnished exactly as they were in 1920, 1940 and 1960, a 1920s garage and two shops – a 1950s general store and a 1930s jeweller's. There is a large playground outside. Open every day from 10 a.m. till 6 p.m.

G There was a village on this site 500 years ago and it is now completely rebuilt. You can walk around the fields and along the paths to see how people lived and worked all those years ago. There is a car park and a large playground. Open every day from 9 a.m. till 5.30 p.m.

H This museum is very small but is full of interesting objects including jewellery, weapons, pottery, cooking equipment and other household items. They were all found on an ancient site outside the town and they are all over 1,000 years old. The museum is open on Saturdays and Sundays only.

Part 3

Questions 11–20

- Look at the statements about the facilities in a hotel.
- Read the text below to decide if each statement is correct or incorrect.
- If it is correct, mark **A on your answer sheet.**
- If it is incorrect, mark **B on your answer sheet.**

Example answer:

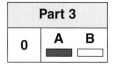

11   Breakfast in the dining room costs the same whatever you eat.

12   The dining room closes at 9 p.m.

13   The Coffee Shop is open the same times as the swimming pool.

14   The receptionist will bring you a newspaper with your breakfast if you want.

15   You can unlock the front door for yourself if you return to the hotel very late.

16   To telephone a room in the hotel, you press 9 followed by the room number.

17   Children may only use the swimming pool when a member of staff is present.

18   You can use the hotel laundry facilities any afternoon.

19   The hotel will look after your money for you while you are out.

20   You must tell the receptionist if you are going out in the evening.

GERALD'S HOTEL   Information

Meals

Breakfast is served in the dining room 7.30–9.30 a.m. (10.00 a.m. on Sundays). Help yourself from our buffet or order a full cooked breakfast at no extra charge. A light breakfast can be served in your room if preferred (see Room Service below).

Dinner is served in the dining room from 7.30 p.m. (Last orders by 9 p.m. please.)

A children's dinner menu is available until 8 p.m. at a reduced charge.

The Coffee Shop at the Swimming Pool is open from 10 a.m. serving a range of drinks, snacks and light meals.

Room service   24-hour room service is not available, but we are happy to bring light meals and snacks to your room for a small extra charge when the Coffee Shop is open. Light breakfasts are also available from 7 a.m. Please inform reception the previous evening if you would like breakfast in your room.

Newspapers can be ordered from Reception and will be on your breakfast table.

We do not have a **night porter**. If you are likely to come back to the hotel after midnight, please ask the receptionist for a front-door key.

The **telephone** in your room can be used to make calls within the hotel by dialling the number as shown on the list beside it. For calls outside, dial 9 followed by the number. Calls are charged at normal price for the first two minutes, then double after that.

The **Swimming Pool** is open from 7 a.m. to 10 p.m. Please collect swimming towels from Reception. Do not use the towels in your bathroom.

Please note that children must be with a responsible adult at all times when using the pool. The hotel does not have staff available to do this and can take no responsibility for accidents.

There is a washing machine (£1.50 required) and drier (50p required). These are in the **laundry room**, opposite Room 17, and are available for guests to use after 1.30 p.m. every day. An iron and ironing board is also available. The hotel also offers a laundry service, which takes a minimum of twenty-four hours, from Monday to Friday. Prices are available from Reception.

Cash and items of value can be locked away in the hotel office if you wish to avoid carrying them with you to the beach etc. Please ask at Reception. There is normally no charge for this service.

Please leave your room by 10 a.m. on the day of your **departure** to give us time to prepare for the next guests. If you would like to leave luggage with us for part of the day, please tell the receptionist the evening before.

Part 4

Questions 21–25

- Read the text and questions below.
- For each question, mark the letter next to the correct answer – **A**, **B**, **C** or **D** – on **your answer sheet**.

Example answer:

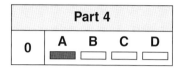

	Part 4			
	A	B	C	D
0	▪	☐	☐	☐

I went to the cinema last week and laughed all the way through the new film *Waiter!* which is set in a restaurant. American actor Tom Waters plays the worst cook the world has ever seen and he employs one of the worst waiters, played by Joe Vermont.

The London restaurant where the filming took place does actually exist. Jane Connors, the owner, runs a successful business and, although she thinks *Waiter!* is a good film, she is very annoyed with the director. When she agreed to the filming, she wasn't told that the film is about a restaurant where everything goes wrong and the food is disgusting. Although the film might make Jane's restaurant famous if it is a success, she is afraid that people will stop coming because they will think the food and service is terrible – like it is in the film. Jane is worried she will lose business and may even have to close and start again with a new restaurant.

Having seen the film, I agree that she has a problem. The film company paid her a very small fee and she has since asked for more. The best solution though is for her to contact the newspapers. I am sure they will be interested in her story and it will actually help her business in the end.

21 What is the writer trying to do in the text?

   A advertise a restaurant

   B review a film

   C explain someone's problem

   D take someone's advice

22 What can the reader find out from the text?

   A why Jane is feeling angry

   B why Jane's restaurant has closed

   C why Jane didn't enjoy the film

   D why Jane's restaurant is unpopular

[Turn over

23 What does the writer think Jane ought to do?

   A open a new restaurant

   B ask the film company for more money

   C improve the quality of the food in her restaurant

   D write to the newspapers

24 What did the director not tell Jane?

   A that the film would be a success

   B that the restaurant in the film would be very bad

   C that she would not be paid

   D that she would need to employ extra staff

25 Which of these is an advert for the film?

   A

> ### *Waiter!*
> Comedy film set in a typical American town.
> Laugh at the mistakes of crazy cook (Tom Waters)
> and mad waiter (Joe Vermont).

   B

> ### *Waiter!*
> Learn how to cook and be amused at the same
> time at this film made specially for television by
> well-known cook, Tom Waters.

   C

> ### *WAITER!*
> *All the action takes place in a famous London
> restaurant. Find out the truth about what happens
> in the kitchens.*

   D

> ### *Waiter!*
> Sit back and enjoy the performances of Tom
> Waters and Joe Vermont in this comedy filmed
> in a London restaurant.

Part 5

Questions 26–35

- Read the text below and choose the correct word for each space.
- For each question, mark the letter next to the correct word – **A**, **B**, **C** or **D** – **on your answer sheet**.

Example answer:

Part 5				
	A	B	C	D
0	■■■	☐	☐	☐

Picasso

If you ask many people to (0) .... a twentieth-century artist, they will suggest 'Picasso'. Although he (26) .... born in 1881 and died in 1973, the general public (27) .... thinks of his work as modern art. His early paintings look traditional (28) .... us nowadays, but his later work is less easy to understand, (29) .... seventy years after he did it. One thing students should (30) .... about Picasso is that he enjoyed a joke. This is clear (31) .... we look at the drawings he made on dishes and pots. When we try to (32) .... the importance of Picasso, we must not forget that he was a clever businessman as well as a great artist. Although poor when young, he was excellent (33) .... selling his work, and he became extremely rich. He believed he was a great artist, and he could (34) .... other people that he was too. Some people feel that there are other twentieth-century artists who should be (35) .... famous, but this can only be decided in the future.

0	**A** name	**B** call	**C** say	**D** tell
26	**A** was	**B** has	**C** is	**D** had
27	**A** yet	**B** still	**C** just	**D** already
28	**A** with	**B** by	**C** to	**D** for
29	**A** all	**B** that	**C** though	**D** even
30	**A** remember	**B** revise	**C** review	**D** remind
31	**A** how	**B** when	**C** where	**D** which
32	**A** check	**B** consist	**C** judge	**D** discover
33	**A** in	**B** on	**C** out	**D** at
34	**A** persuade	**B** insist	**C** decide	**D** agree
35	**A** actually	**B** presently	**C** fairly	**D** equally

Writing

Part 1

Questions 1–5

- Here are some sentences about a new shopping centre.
- For each question, finish the second sentence so that it means the same as the first.
- The second sentence is started for you. **Write only the missing words on your answer sheet.**
- You may use this page for any rough work.

Example: A famous actor opened the new shopping centre last week.

The new shopping centre _was opened by a famous actor last week._

1   Usually I get bored when I go shopping.

Usually I find shopping ....

2   But last week I spent five hours in the new shopping centre.

But last week I was in the new shopping centre ....

3   I prefer the new shopping centre to the old one.

I like the new shopping centre better ....

4   I didn't have enough money to buy the shoes I wanted.

The shoes I wanted were ....

5   Parking is difficult unless you arrive early.

Parking is easy ....

Part 2

Questions 6–15

- You want to find an English penfriend through an international magazine.
- The magazine sends you an application form to complete.
- Look at the form and answer each question.
- **Write your answers on your answer sheet.**
- You may use this page for any rough work.

International Language Exchange

Application for English Penfriend

Full name: (**6**) ....

First language: (**7**) ....

Age: (**8**) ....

Sex: (**9**) ....

Home address (including country): (**10**) ....

....

Please give the name of your favourite school subject, or of your job: (**11**) ....

....

How often would you like to exchange letters with your penfriend? (**12**) ....

....

What are your main indoor and outdoor leisure activities? (**13**) ....

....

What type of holiday do you prefer? (**14**) ....

....

Signature: (**15**) ....

Part 3

Question 16

- A friend of yours had a birthday party last week.
- Now you are writing a letter to an English-speaking friend about the party.
- Tell your friend what you did at the party, describe the present you took your friend and say who you met there.
- **Finish the letter on your answer sheet, using about 100 words.**

Dear . . . . . ,

I want to tell you about the party I went to last week. ....

....

You must write your answers on
the separate answer sheet.

Part 1

Questions 1–7

- There are seven questions in this Part.
- For each question there are four pictures and a short recording.
- You will hear each recording twice.
- For each question, look at the pictures and listen to the recording.
- Choose the correct picture and put a tick (✓) in the box below it.

Example: Which train will the woman catch?

   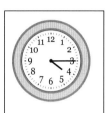

A ☐   B ☐   C ✓   D ☐

1   Which band did the boy watch last night?

A ☐   B ☐   C ☐   D ☐

2   Where is the woman's new flat?

A ☐   B ☐   C ☐   D ☐

[Turn over

3 Where will they meet?

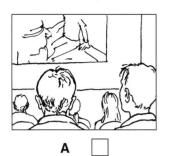 **A** ☐

 **B** ☐

 **C** ☐

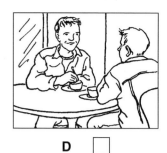 **D** ☐

4 Which is the boy's teacher?

 **A** ☐

 **B** ☐

 **C** ☐

 **D** ☐

5 Which photograph are they looking at?

 **A** ☐

 **B** ☐

 **C** ☐

 **D** ☐

6 What time is the flight from New York expected?

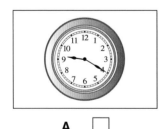 **A** ☐

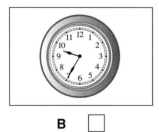 **B** ☐

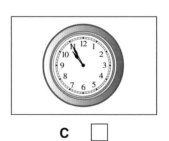 **C** ☐

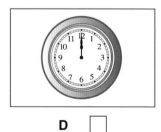 **D** ☐

7 What was the boy doing when the phone rang?

 **A** ☐

 **B** ☐

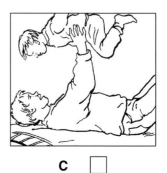 **C** ☐

 **D** ☐

Part 2

Questions 8–13

- Look at the questions for this Part.
- You will hear a woman talking to an evening class about carpentry.
- Put a tick (✓) in the correct box for each question.

8   The speaker says that when she was at school, girls

A ☐ were taught separately from boys.

B ☐ could do carpentry if they wanted to.

C ☐ were not interested in carpentry.

D ☐ were not allowed to do carpentry.

9   Making her chest of drawers took

A ☐ eigthteen months.

B ☐ six months.

C ☐ two months.

D ☐ one week.

10   She first planned to put the chest of drawers

A ☐ in the kitchen.

B ☐ in the sitting room.

C ☐ in the hall.

D ☐ in the bedroom.

11   What advice does she give about electric tools?

A ☐ They are useful for some people.

B ☐ They are necessary for beginners.

C ☐ Only lazy people use them.

D ☐ Cheap ones are dangerous.

12   She suggests that the first job should be something

A ☐ really useful.

B ☐ small and simple.

C ☐ for a friend.

D ☐ which practises many skills.

13   What does she suggest that the class should do first?

A ☐ choose who they will work with

B ☐ buy the right tools

C ☐ decide what they need for one job

D ☐ discuss what they should do

Part 3

Questions 14–19

- Look at the notes about a fashion show.
- Some information is missing.
- You will hear someone talking on the radio about the fashion show.
- For each question, fill in the missing information in the numbered space.

Fashion Show

Place: sports stadium

Date: **(14)** ....

Time: 7.30

Colour of clothes: grey or **(15)** ....

Talk: at 6.30 by a **(16)** ....

Clothes for sale: everything except **(17)** ....

Prize for best design: **(18)** ....

Buses: depart at 6p.m. and 7 p.m. from outside **(19)** ....

Part 4

Questions 20–25

- Look at the six statements for this Part.
- You will hear a conversation between a boy, Ian, and a girl, Zoe, about a holiday.
- Decide if you think each statement is correct or incorrect.
- If you think it is correct, put a tick (✓) in the box under **A** for **YES**. If you think it is not correct, put a tick (✓) in the box under **B** for **NO**.

		A YES	B NO
20	Ian is going to visit relatives who live in Africa.	☐	☐
21	Zoe believes Namibia is a good place to visit.	☐	☐
22	Ian's parents insist he must go on holiday with them.	☐	☐
23	Zoe's father is unemployed.	☐	☐
24	Zoe's mother dislikes flying.	☐	☐
25	Ian suggests Zoe should visit Namibia with him.	☐	☐

Part 1

General conversation: saying who you are, asking for and giving personal information, spelling

You imagine you don't know each other. The examiner directs you to ask each other questions to find out some information about each other.

Ask each other at least four of these questions:

- What's your name? Can you spell your surname for me?
- Where do you live?
- Is that near the city centre?
- Do you live in a house or a flat?
- Is it very old? Do you know when it was built?
- How many rooms does it have?
- Have you always lived there?

Part 2

Simulated situation: exchanging opinions, saying what you think other people would like

The examiner gives you both a picture. You do a task together.

A friend has asked you to look after her 5-year-old son, Sam, next Saturday afternoon and you need to decide what you will do with him. Look at page 151. There is a picture of Sam and ideas of places to go. Decide together where you will take Sam. You will only have time to do two things. Ask and answer questions like these:

- What do you think he likes doing?
- Would he prefer to be indoors or outside?
- What kind of food do you think he likes?
- Will he get too tired / bored doing that?

Part 3

Responding to photographs: describing a room and the things in it, saying where things are, talking about other people

You take turns to tell each other about a photograph.

Candidate A: look at photograph 5A on page 154.
Candidate B: look at photograph 5B on page 156.

Think about your photograph for a few seconds. Describe it to your partner for about one minute. Tell your partner about these things:

- what kind of place it is
- what you can see (furniture, objects, etc.)
- whether it looks tidy or untidy
- what you can guess about the owner.

Part 4

General conversation about the photographs: talking about likes, dislikes and and your habits

The examiner asks you to talk to your partner.

Tell each other about your room at home. Use these ideas.

- Describe your room and say if you are happy with it as it is or if you would like to change it. Say what you would change.
- Say what things you like to have in your room.
- Say if you think your room shows what kind of person you are.

Extra practice for Writing Part 1

1 ▶ a) **For each sentence, finish the second sentence so that it means the same as the first. As you do each sentence, think about the language it is testing.**

1 You're too young to come to the disco.
   You're not ....

2 May we leave our bikes here?
   Are we ....?

3 Is this jacket too small for me?
   Is this jacket big ....?

4 I'm better at skiing than you are.
   You're not ....

5 Can children go on these rides?
   Is it ....?

6 This book is more interesting than that one.
   That book isn't ....

7 This water isn't cool enough.
   This water is too ....

8 You are advised to take this medicine with a glass of water.
   You should ....

9 This house is close to the sports ground.
   This house isn't ....

10 I like coffee better than tea.
   I prefer coffee ....

11 My bedroom is above the sitting room.
   The sitting room is ....

12 These jeans aren't clean enough to wear.
   These jeans are too ....

13 This shop is closed on Saturday afternoons.
   This shop isn't ....

14 It's essential to rest until your leg is better.
   You ....

15 Their house isn't as big as yours.
   Your house is ....

16 The weather is too bad for us to go out.
   The weather isn't ....

17 My suitcase was on top of my sister's.
   My sister's suitcase was ....

18 It isn't necessary to pay if you're a student.
   You ....

19   I'm not as pretty as my sister.

   My sister is ....

20   A very tall man sat in front of me at the theatre.

   I sat ....

b)   **Look at the sentences again. Four language points are tested. Put the sentences
into four groups. Can you give each group a name? (These are some of the
language points you often find tested in Writing Part 1.)**

2 ▶ a)   **For each sentence, finish the second sentence so that it means the same as
the first. As you do each sentence, think about the language it is testing.**

1   The parcels were delivered to the wrong address.

   The postman ....

2   There are plenty of chairs in the meeting room.

   The meeting room ....

3   He asked where the children could play.

   'Where ....?'

4   These vegetables must be kept in the freezer.

   You must ....

5   My school will have a new computer department next year.

   Next year, there ....

6   The bus was delayed by an accident.

   An accident ....

7   She explained she hadn't got any money.

   She said, 'I ....,'

8   There weren't any grapes at the greengrocer's.

   The greengrocer ....

9   We said we were looking for our books.

   We said, 'We ....,'

10   This box should not be opened in bright sunshine.

   Don't ....

11   The swimming pool had lots of modern equipment.

   At the swimming pool, there ....

12   I told him he had to pay immediately.

   I said, 'You ....,'

13   There may be some cheap clothes in this shop.

   This shop may ....

14   You asked me to book four seats for the show.

   You said, 'Please ....,'

15   The new museum will be opened by the Prime Minister.

   The Prime Minister ....

b)   **Look at the sentences again. Three language points are tested. Put the sentences
into three groups. Can you give each group a name? (These are some of the
language points you often find tested in Writing Part 1.)**

Visuals for Speaking Test

Test 1, Part 2

Useful language

What about ...?

I'd prefer to ...

I enjoy ...

How much ...?

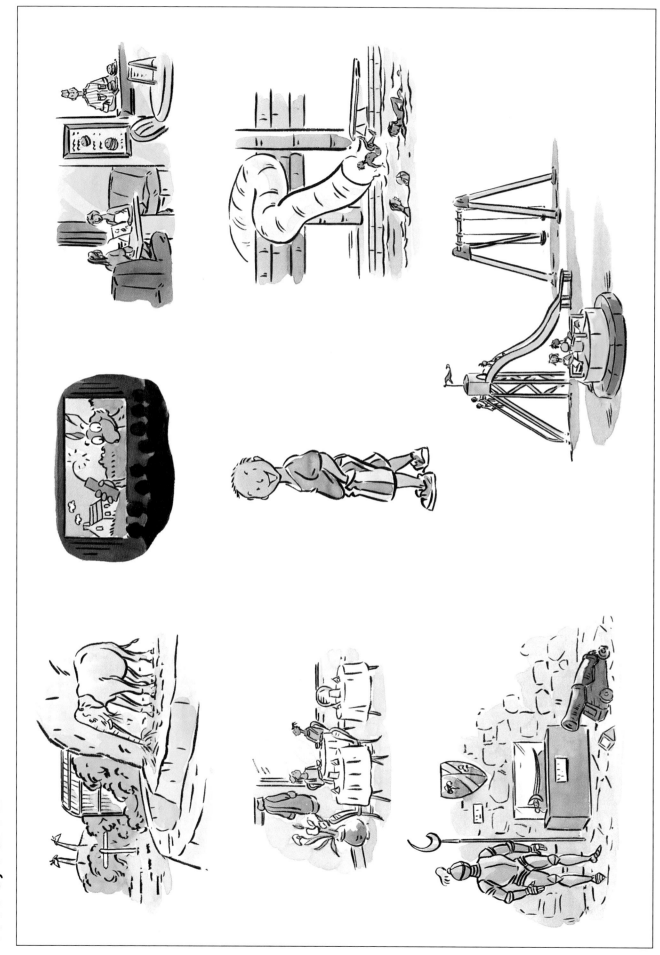

Test 1, Part 3

Test 2, Part 3

Test 3, Part 3

3A

Test 4, Part 3

4A

Test 5, Part 3

Test 1, Part 3

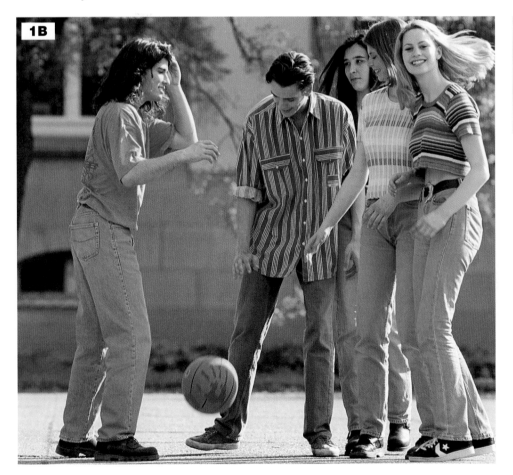

Useful language

There's …
I think they're …
They look …
I think he / she …
In the distance …

Test 2, Part 3

2B

Useful language

I think it's …
They look …
They might be …
At the back of the room …
At the front there's …

Test 3, Part 3

3B

Test 4, Part 3

Test 5, Part 3

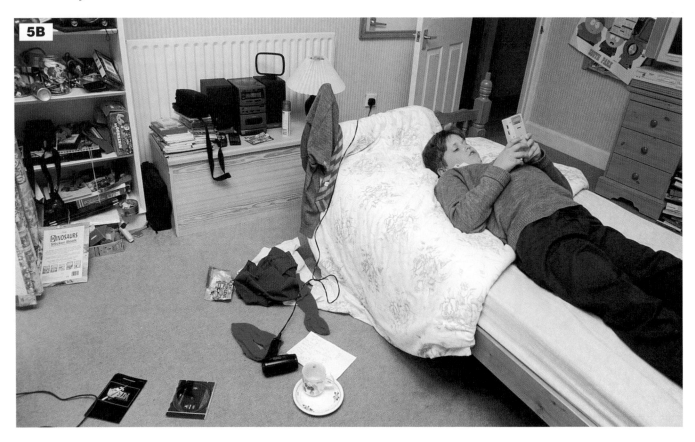

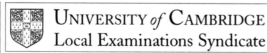
UNIVERSITY *of* CAMBRIDGE
Local Examinations Syndicate

SAMPLE

Candidate Name
If not already printed, write name in CAPITALS and complete the Candidate No. grid (in pencil).

Candidate's signature

Examination Title

Centre

Supervisor:
[X] If the candidate is ABSENT or has WITHDRAWN shade here ▭

Centre No.

Candidate No.

Examination Details

0	0	0	0
1	1	1	1
2	2	2	2
3	3	3	3
4	4	4	4
5	5	5	5
6	6	6	6
7	7	7	7
8	8	8	8
9	9	9	9

PET Reading and Writing - Answer Sheet 1

Reading

Use a pencil.

Mark one letter for each question.

Example:
If you think A is the right answer to the question, mark your answer sheet like this:

| 0 | A | B | C | D |

Rub out any answer you want to change, with an eraser.

Part 1	Part 2	Part 3	Part 4	Part 5
1 A B C D	6 A B C D E F G H	11 A B	21 A B C D	26 A B C D
2 A B C D	7 A B C D E F G H	12 A B	22 A B C D	27 A B C D
3 A B C D	8 A B C D E F G H	13 A B	23 A B C D	28 A B C D
4 A B C D	9 A B C D E F G H	14 A B	24 A B C D	29 A B C D
5 A B C D	10 A B C D E F G H	15 A B	25 A B C D	30 A B C D
		16 A B		31 A B C D
		17 A B		32 A B C D
		18 A B		33 A B C D
		19 A B		34 A B C D
		20 A B		35 A B C D

Continue on the other side of this sheet ➝

PETRW-1

DP396/329

Writing (Parts 1 and 2)

Write your answer clearly in the space provided.

SAMPLE

Part 1: Write your answers below.	Do not write here
1	1
2	2
3	3
4	4
5	5

Part 2: Write your answers below.	Do not write here
6	6
7	7
8	8
9	9
10	10
11	11
12	12
13	13
14	14
15	15

Put your answer to Writing Part 3 on Answer Sheet 2 ⟶

Part 3: Write your answer in the box below.

This section for use by SECOND Examiner only

Marks:

Task	0	1	2	3	4	5

Language	0	1	2	3	4	5

Examiner Number

0	1	2	3	4	5	6	7	8	9
0	1	2	3	4	5	6	7	8	9
0	1	2	3	4	5	6	7	8	9
0	1	2	3	4	5	6	7	8	9

SAMPLE

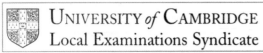

UNIVERSITY *of* CAMBRIDGE
Local Examinations Syndicate

SAMPLE

Candidate Name
If not already printed, write name
in CAPITALS and complete the
Candidate No. grid (in pencil).

Candidate's signature ....

Examination Title

Centre

Supervisor:

[X] If the candidate is ABSENT or has WITHDRAWN shade here ▭

Centre No.

Candidate No.

Examination Details

0	0	0	0
1	1	1	1
2	2	2	2
3	3	3	3
4	4	4	4
5	5	5	5
6	6	6	6
7	7	7	7
8	8	8	8
9	9	9	9

PET Listening Answer Sheet

• You must transfer all your answers from the Listening Question Paper to this answer sheet.

Use a pencil

For Parts 1,2 and 4: Mark one letter for each question.

For example, if you think A is the right answer to
the question, mark your answer sheet like this:

| 0 | A̲ |

Change your answer
like this:

For Part 3: Write your answers in the spaces
next to the numbers (14 - 19) like this:

| 0 | *example* | | ▭ 0 ▭ |

	Part 1		Part 2		Part 3	Do not write here		Part 4
1	A B C D	8	A B C D	14		▭ 14 ▭	20	A B
2	A B C D	9	A B C D	15		▭ 15 ▭	21	A B
3	A B C D	10	A B C D	16		▭ 16 ▭	22	A B
4	A B C D	11	A B C D	17		▭ 17 ▭	23	A B
5	A B C D	12	A B C D	18		▭ 18 ▭	24	A B
6	A B C D	13	A B C D	19		▭ 19 ▭	25	A B
7	A B C D							

PET-L

DP312/86